THE
INTERORGANIZATIONAL
COMMUNITY

THE
INTERORGANIZATIONAL
COMMUNITY

Robert C. Anderson

The Edwin Mellen Press
Lewiston/Queenston/Lampeter

Library of Congress Cataloging-in-Publication Data

Anderson, Robert C.
    The interorganizational community / by Robert C. Anderson.
       p.   cm.
    Includes bibliographical references.
    ISBN 0-7734-9300-X
    1. Community. 2. Community development. 3. Interorganizational
relations. I. Title.
HM131.A458 1993
307--dc20   93-1353
                                         CIP

A CIP catalog record for this book
is available from the British Library.

The Edwin Mellen Press
Box 450
Lewiston, New York
USA 14092

The Edwin Mellen Press
Box 67
Queenston, Ontario
CANADA L0S 1L0

Edwin Mellen Press, Ltd.
Lampeter, Dyfed, Wales
UNITED KINGDOM SA48 7DY

Printed in the United States of America

To Barbara
My Wife

CONTENTS

List of Figures   xi

Preface   xv

Chapter

1   The Community   1
        Introduction   1
        Community Theories   4
        Social Systems   6
        Independent-Interdependent Community   10
        Contemporary Communities   11
        The Questioning Community   13
        The Community of Conflict   14
        Planned Community Interaction   15
        Community as a Social System   18

2   The Society   21
        Structural Theories   21
        Theory of Structuration   24
        Theories of Fragmentation of Consciousness   28
        The Metronomic Society   29
        The Cooperative Value Process   31

3   The Organization   37
        Social Rule Systems Theory   39
        Boundaries of Organizational Systems   40
        Note of Concern   41
        Perceptual Theory and Organization   42

What is an Organization 43
Organization as a Social System 44
Organization as a System of Planned Change 47
Social Power and the Demand for Its Control 48
Organization Life Cycle 51
Birth Period 51
Growth Period 53
Maturity Period 54
Decline and Death Period 55
Entrepreneurial and Innovative Spirit for the Future 56

4 The Environment 59
System Formation and Dependency 60
Environmental Dependency 65
Rule and Belief Systems 66
Individuals and Their Organizational Environment 67
Mega-Crisis and Environment 68
Climate and Culture 70

5 Organizations and Interorganization Relations 73
The Individual and the Organization 74
Private-Public Relationships 76
Coalition Dependency 77
The Spiral-Lineal Concept of Social Organization 78
Collaboration in Our Turbulent Environment 79
Networks and Coalitions 83

6 Community Cooperation and Involvement 87
A Phenomenological Start 88
The Cooperative Process 91
The Involvement Process 93
Winding It Up 102

7 The Democratic Model of Participation Examined 105
The New Look 110
The Returns Model 116

8	How to Organize for Inventiveness	119
	A Development Organization	127
	The Michigan Livestock Health Council	127
	The IACD Committee	129
	IACD Committee Report Format	132
	IACD Subcommittees	134
	The Council Proper	135
	The Council's Operation	136
	Michigan Livestock Health Council Objectives	138
	How the Council Worked	139
9	A Technique for Predicting Intraorganizational Action	143
	Characteristics of Organizational Systems	147
	The Theory to Be Used	150
	Population and Sampling Procedures	153
	Element Identification and Measurement	153
	The Open-Ended Question (OEQ) Device	154
	Administration of the OEQ Device	156
	Analysis and Classification of Responses	157
	The Rating Scale (RS) Device	158
	Summary	162
10	A Sociometric Approach to the Analysis of Interorganizational Relationships	165
	Application of the Approach to Economic Development of a Region	168
	Universe Selection	170
	Sociometric Instrumentation	173
	Sociometric Analysis of Interorganizational Data	173
	Interaction Structures	176
	Constellation Sets	184
	Constellation Memberships	184
	Linkages between Constellation Sets	185
	Influence Patterns	186
	Status Arrangements	187
	Analysis by Homogeneous Groupings	192
	Conclusions	199

11   An Interorganizational Approach to the Explanation
     of Community Development Activities   205
          An Interorganizational Explanation of Community
          Development Activities   209
          Interorganizational Action Is Required
          for Collective Community Decisions   210
          The Adoption of an Innovative Idea at
          the Community Level   213
          Coupling of Interests   217
          A Case in Point   223
          Relationships between Organizations Classified
          by Goals and the Organizational Conditions
          Favorable for the Adoption of Innovative Ideas   224
          The Relationship between Power Used and
          the Adoption Orientation of Members
          to Innovative Ideas   230
          Summary and Conclusion   233

     Bibliography   235

LIST OF FIGURES

Figure

1   Key concepts of structuration theory and
    functionalism compared   27

2   Input-output model of organization action   47

3   Demand for control—a general model   50

4   Organizational demand for control model   52

5   Model for community involvement   95

6   Increasing returns   113

7   Diminishing returns   115

8   The returns model   116

9   A model of development organization activity   122

10 Relationship of the Inter-Agency College Department
    (IACD) committee to its environment   130

11 Organization chart of the Michigan Livestock Health
    Council   137

12 A sample of the Open-Ended Question (OEQ) device   154

13   A sample Rating Scale (RS) device   160

14   The perceived organized structure of the transportation
      interest sector of Michigan's Upper Peninsula by county   172

15   Interorganizational sociometric instrument   175

16   Rank ordered organizational sociometric scores
      received and given by related organizations in
      Michigan's Upper Peninsula in response to the
      question, "What organization does your organization
      deal with in carrying out its business?"   178-179

17   Matrix representation of constellations formed based
      on reciprocal choices of 61 selected organizations in
      response to the question, "What organization does
      your organization deal with in carrying out its
      business?"   180-181

18   Constellation sets of 61 selected organizations in
      21 constellations formed in response to the question,
      "What organization does your organization deal with
      in carrying out its business?"   182-183

19   Constellation sets and membership scores of 61
      selected organizations in 21 constellations formed
      in response to the question, "What organization
      does your organization deal with in carrying out
      its business?"   190-191

20   Sociometric scores given and received by specified
      interest sectors in Michigan's Upper Peninsula in
      response to the question, "What organization does
      your organization deal with in carrying out its
      business?"   193

21 Sociogram reflecting perceived high interaction among interest sectors in Michigan's Upper Peninsula in response to the question, "What organization does your organization deal with in carrying out its business?"   196

22 A model for the adoption of an innovative idea in a community   214-215

23 Involvement patterns of relevant order organizations in the implementation of an innovative idea at the community level   221

24 Typologies of conditions for organizational adoption relationships   225

25 Typologies of compliance relation of members to the adoption of an innovative idea   231

PREFACE

What makes a community tick? How does it work? Can we work with a community in such a way as to enhance the positive and reduce the negative aspects of community life? These are a few of the questions a group of scholars from Michigan State University asked themselves in the 1950s as they tried to find an effective way to extend MSU's land-grant philosophy of education into the places Michiganians lived, worked, and enjoyed. Because, as one administrator observed, "universities have departments and communities have problems," the group realized that a traditional single-discipline approach could not work. Finally, their deliberations resulted in the formation of a multi-disciplinary, applied research, and consulting unit within the university called the Institute for Community Development.

My search for an understanding of community began in earnest when I joined the Institute and became part of a staff that included people from the fields of anthropology, geography, urban planning, community development, law, education, accounting, engineering, political science, law enforcement, and theater. Our mission was to extend access and use of the university's knowledge to Michigan citizens as they went about the daily problem-solving activities that are normal to creating, maintaining, and redeveloping communities. We operated through inter- and multidisciplinary research, consultation, workshops, seminars, and publications, working in specific places and on particular issues viewed as important to the citizens of Michigan who were working to make their communities better.

My image of what communities are was first influenced by mentors Christopher Sower, Paul Miller, and Duane Gibson, sociologists all, who taught me that the interaction of people and their organizations is what communities are about and that a clear understanding of that phenomenon would stand me in good stead. This book represents my image of community after over 35 years spent aggressively securing an understanding and explanation of this most outstanding human endeavor called community.

The first part of the book deals with literature on community and community development as presented by philosophers, theorists, researchers, and practitioners. Chapter 1 presents an historical view of community as seen by scholars across time, from Plato to Warren. Communities are viewed in many ways, from ideal states of perfect unit to interacting, locally relevant social systems that endure over time.

In Chapter 2 the broader notions of community from a society perspective are examined. Gidden's theory of structuration and Young's cyclical theory of the metronomic society dominate as ways to explain what communities are and how they form, sustain and reproduce themselves, and dissolve. Societies and communities are viewed as cooperatives that bring distributive justice and balance to individuals and groups.

Chapter 3 deals with the organization, which is presented as a basic human invention enabling the individual to fully develop as a human being. We are, in large measure, what organizations expect us to be. Organizations provide us with structure, rules, boundaries, control, and values by which we live. Organizations and their inevitable specialization and division of labor teach us the value of dependency. For, as we discover in Chapter 5, an organization is not sufficient in and of itself, but rather is dependent on coalitions and a series of interorganizational networks for its very survival. All individuals, organizations, coalitions, and networks, as noted in Chapter 4, are also dependent on another factor, which is completely out of their direct control, the environment. Interestingly enough, while the environment of an organization takes in everything around an organization, including weather, the most turbulent environmental force is found to be that of other organizations.

Organizations, communities, and societies all exhibit great dependency on cooperation and involvement. In Chapter 6 I present the idea that cooperation is neither inherently good or bad, but may be either or both depending on the situation. Three postulates stating sufficient conditions to cause a person or organization to cooperate is followed by a detail model for community involvement that traces the process of how a cooperative involvement is taken.

The balance of the book contains case studies that I have carried out over the years to illustrate ways to apply theory in explaining, understanding, and, in some cases, solving specific problems common to communities. In Chapter 7, for example, I discuss the question of how much citizen or democratic participation in decision making should there be when community issues are to be solved. The issue is approached with the use of a *returns model* that indicates the kinds of decisions that result from increasing participation in decision making. The Economic Opportunity and Model Cities programs were the case studied.

The Michigan Livestock Health Council case, Chapter 8, shows how a large number of independent organizations reallocated some of their resources to a development organization, without merging or consolidating units, to achieve goals no one unit could have achieved independently. In order to determine the aspirations of members for such a diverse and broad organization, I developed a two-stage technique to assess their wishes (Chapter 9). We needed efficient reliable tools, easy and economical to use, that allowed respondents to express themselves freely and concisely. The Open-Ended Question and the Rating-Scale devices transform members' statements about the organization to interval-scaled measurements of consensus variation about specific elements of the organization.

Coalition and network studies of eleven economic sectors in Michigan's Upper Peninsula, discussed in Chapter 10, demonstrate the power of using sociometric techniques at the organizational level. Everyday business linkages and dependency relationships between 61 organizations representing eleven interest sectors of the area were identified and explained. From such information, predictions as to specific organization and coalition influence are made.

Finally, in Chapter 11, an interorganizational theory to account for and explain the adoption and implementation of innovative ideas at the community level is presented. A flow model of predicted organizational response and a model of how organizations couple or come together in support or opposition to the idea is presented. The adoption and implementation of a no-smoking ordinance in East Lansing, Michigan, is the case used to test the theory.

It is my hope that readers of this book will find it to be provocative, reliable, and useful.

This book would not have been possible had it not been for the dedication, support, and assistance of Barbara Anderson, my wife. It also is the result of the extensive and able assistance provided by Nancy Gendell, Shawn Lock, and Cheryl Lowe. Special thanks go to Frank Fear, the Department of Resource Development, and Michigan State University for their support.

I am grateful for permission to quote material I had published earlier in the journals *Clinical Sociology Review, Sociological Practice: Community Development and Other Community Applications*, and the *Journal of the Community Development Society*; and in *Interorganizational Relations*, a collection of essays issued by Penguin Books.

Chapter 1

THE COMMUNITY

I am convinced communal life can flourish only if it exists for an aim outside itself. Community is viable if it is the outgrowth of a deep involvement in a purpose which is other than, or above, that of being a community (Bettleheim 1974).

Introduction

The term "community" has many meanings, but historically humankind has viewed it as an ideal of perfect unity such as that described by Plato and Jean Jacques Rosseau. Both envisioned societies that would join people as full and authentic human beings, not as parts shaped to fit an external order. Tinder (1980) argues that while this notion of community is alluring to maintain, such a community is unattainable in a stable form because of obstacles that are natural, moral, and axiological resulting from man's natural and ontological situation. According to Scherer (1972, 12), "The word 'community' is emotionally tinged. It is usually equated with a condition of happiness.

At best, community provides meaning and purpose to life, but at worst, community can be a source of tyranny and inhumanity."

"Community is the fundamental theme of man together as opposed to man alone" (Scherer 1972, 1). Community is a synonym for togetherness and love, which, in Tonnies'(1988) view, was life organically and unselfishly bound with the lives of others. But it is also a unit of social and territorial organization in which people live, work, attend church and school, and carry on a host of other activities that are a part of daily living. According to Poplin (1972), communities are unique in that all of a person's needs can potentially be met within them. This concept has permeated scholarly literature of community over time, but if that were all community is, a community would be nothing more than the John Hancock building in Chicago where workplace, leisure activities, entertainment, health accommodations, residence, and all other basic human needs for modern life are provided for in one building (Williams 1989).

Poplin (1979) refers to community as those units of society and territorial organization that, depending on size, are called hamlets, villages, towns, and cities--places where people maintain homes, earn a living, rear children, and carry on most life activities. It is a network of interaction between individuals as well as groups, organizations, and institutions. Its basic social processes are cooperation, competition, and conflict.

Historically it has generally been held that all communities are composed of people who are members of social interacting units with common ties, values, beliefs, sentiments, attitudes, goals, and language bounded by geographic areas (Zorbaugh 1929). But modern scholars Poplin (1979) and Newman (1981) called into question this view of community. They argue that given the heterogeneity, complexity, and geographic dispersion of environmental forces that directly affect people's lives in a given location at a given time, this definition of community is no longer valid. Are we dealing only with semantic differences or something else? I believe it is not semantic differences but more a case of specific yet different definitions and changing perceptions among scholars of community life who attempt to explain aspects of this human phenomenon over time. No conceptualization is complete of itself, nor can it be because of the limitation of the human mind to comprehend the whole of anything.

Tonnies' (1988) distinction between community and society is put in terms of *Gemeinschaft* and *Gesellschaft*. Gemeinschaft refers to people in community with shared norms and values, frequent contacts, and warm personal relationships — people with a sense of belonging to a community where there are few changes from generation to generation. Community is understood as in a primitive tribe. Gesellschaft refers to people in places like cities where change is the norm, where there is little consensus on values or norms, and where impersonal contacts are the norm not the exception.

In the city individuals seem to replace group loyalty, anonymity is preferred, and mechanics, order, and the calculated unity of a modern factory seem to be the preferred social order. The Gemeinschaft view

of people interacting together is really a yearning for community in which
life is organically and unselfishly bound with the lives of others.   A
utopia.

Community Theories

Wild (1981) has presented a series of summaries of community
theories and studies that include most, if not all, of the classics from
1930 to 1980.   It is an excellent bibliography and summary of major
theoretical and empirical works of community and society.   In the early
years, descriptive studies were most prevalent.   From 1950-1960
positivism and methodological approaches dominated the literature. This
decade produced studies where methodology and the logical procedures
of the natural and physical sciences were fashionable. From 1960-1970
positivism was attacked by phenomenologicalists and neo-Marxists.
They began investigating the assumptions and meanings held and used
by individuals in everyday life.   The neo-Marxists, in fact, challenged all
forms of positivism, especially 'value-free science', and place or location
domination.   They placed greater emphasis on utopian and economic
analysis.

Today Wild believes that the deterministic theories of phenomenology and neo-Marxism, which claim to explain total reality don't. These
theories do not achieve their goal in part because the human mind simply
cannot grasp the total.   As such, any new idea that emerges is limited
and partial in nature and its meaning is only relevant to the observers
and their values.   This is true for philosophers, theorists, scholars, and

the ordinary people living in a place called community. It is for that reason Wild, and I, prefer to use various models of community and to develop useful but limited generalizations about community over time. I do find myself giving special importance to some concepts over others, any or all that will add meaning and understanding to me as the observer. This is no doubt based on my own perceptions, values, experiences, and interest at any specific time of my inquiry.

In her review of community studies, theories, and philosophies, Effrat (1974), as do I, noted that scholars in each tradition make assumptions that either an entity is or isn't a community according to their own personal criteria; for example, if it is not territorially grounded, it isn't a community; if there are no common beliefs and values or if it doesn't have common institutions, it isn't a community, etc. Yet these seemingly contradictory or incomplete approaches to the study of community do provide valuable and complementary information on what constitutes a community. Effrat concluded that in any case aspects of community can be viewed as multidimensional ordinal variables that vary with specific values or position in a series. For her and me, things are communities not by redefinition but by empirical investigation and perception of events. Such phenomena may be viewed as multi-dimensional ordinal variables that are never all-inclusive but they do provide a degree of understanding of what is "communityness" in any given situation at any given time.

Social Systems

Poplin (1979) raises the notion of social system theory and functionalism as a way to explain community. For him the community is the major social system, containing subsystems called the institutions of government, economy, education, religion, and family. Each of these subsystems, in turn, is composed of a variety of social and/or associated groups. Statuses of each member or position of members in these groups are viewed as the basic building blocks out of which social groups are structured. The individual becomes a part of these groups and hence a member of larger social systems by playing the roles attached to these statuses.

Plant (1974), on the other hand, tends to view community as fact and value. As such, community is what makes persons whole as they engage as participating community members. This theory of community is used to show how individual self-fulfillment is dependent on the community organization, not vice versa. Discrete spheres of cooperation and competition between special organized interests arise out of the division of labor that occurs. This functional notion of community encapsulates the values of individuals only in a social setting. The social interaction that evolves from shared convictions and rules of governance that are formed link directly to the idea of authority, which is seen as a necessary condition of organizational as well as community existence.

Modern thinkers such as Newman (1981) today see communities of interest that are more dense, smaller in scale, and more closely juxtaposed with others than we would first expect. Newman argues the

more divergent the interacting culture, the greater the need for commonly accepted decorum for encounter or rules for acceptable social
behavior. The old concept of community based on a grouping of people
united by a common background, similarity of pursuits, and physical
proximity has given way to communities of people sharing similar
interests but for different reasons and sometimes even separated by
physical distance.

Gusfield (1975) uses the idea of "system" to characterize
concepts of community and society. For him community refers not to
location but to the quality or character of human relationships. How
members cooperate, conflict, and bond is what unites or differentiates
the members of community. These are the important community
properties used to understand, explain and predict community-like
phenomenon. For Gusfield, Effrat, and me, community is viewed as
more than one kind of a concept on a lineal path, and certainly it is not
totally explained in scientific concepts. For example, concepts embody-
ing generalization expressing a belief in the incompatibility between
forms of human association, as perspectives used to make the community experience possible, are not purely scientific in nature.

Roberts (1979) notes a linkage between communities and their
environments by defining community as a collection of people who have
become aware of some problem or some goal and have formulated a
group objective to achieve the goal. This view is different from
traditional community theory in that such a group of people can be from

distant places, and can be a relatively small group of people forming an organization or system, dedicated only to achieve a common goal.

Robert's notion links nicely into Loomis' (1960) concept of systematic linkage that is the process whereby one or more of the elements of at least two social systems are articulated in a manner that for some purposes and on some occasions may be viewed as one. Some of the elements to be linked are beliefs, knowledge, feeling, and sentiment.

Observable characteristics of the community system are important considerations in the study of community action. Moe (1959) lists some of these characteristics as follows:

* The community is a system of systems.

* The community is not structurally and functionally centralized.

* The development of a "planned change" program in most communities involves many unforeseen pressures, actions, and interactions among the sources of active change power.

* Communication of feelings and ideas among people in different groups and organizations in most communities is difficult and relatively infrequent. As a result, serious misunderstandings among groups exist and others are allowed to develop.

* There generally is no adequate mechanism in most communities for the settlement of intergroup differences or the achievement of understanding among members of different groups. The community generally has no way through

which policies and programs affecting the whole community can be integrated.

*   Members of the several groups and subcultures represented in the community know little about the control systems of each other or other groups and such frequently make unrealistic demands on members of these groups.

*   Groups rarely follow an action evaluation or an experimental methodology in meeting their problems. Too frequently problems are predefined to fit special categories or stereotypes.

*   The objectives, programs, and activities of various groups are often interpreted by members of the groups as mutually threatening. Such perception arises because groups are unable to distinguish problem solving from their own personal problems, processes of maintaining membership and keeping active in their organizations.

*   Leaders as well as members of organizations and groups do not see or understand each other realistically. The differences between group or member roles that are defined from within the group by members, and those attributed by members of other groups are generally great enough to seriously impede effective cooperation between such groups.

*   The advantages of cooperation, nonetheless, are generally recognized. Facilities are lacking, however, to implement this recognition.

These relationships found within communities need to be recognized in order that a sound program of change or action may be developed. The job of those who would change communities is primarily one of bridging the gaps wherever possible and in this way obtain sufficient cooperative effort.

Chekki (1990), in his discussions of theoretical, methodological, and empirical research of micro and macro social linkages, advocates the use of cross-cultural, comparative, and interdisciplinary analysis of community structure and change. He notes that community is really a society in miniature. It is the socio-cultural milieu in which people live, spend most of their time, and satisfy most of their needs. Next to the family, community is the place where our primary personal experiences take place. Community is a key concept for us in order to understand social life. It is an important predictor of most aspects we refer to as quality of life.

Independent-Interdependent Community

Silverman and her colleagues (1989) note that the structure of common interests found in communities make interdependence among neighbors both explicit and unavoidable. Some folks try to avoid this fact by relying on voluntary organizations, elected, or self-appointed persons to represent their common interests. Some common-interest members of communities, such as apartment dwellers, young singles, retirees, private entrepreneurs, homeowners, often fail to participate in the public affairs of their vested common interest as expected. This is true because they generally do not trust their perceived independently held rights to a common-interest representative and are not willing or able to do everything themselves. In today's world, common-interest interdependence seems to have given way to the more culturally based perceived and derived independence of interest. Our perceived individual rights such as property ownership, dominates our behavior. This gives analysts of community fits. How can we talk about community—i.e., people together—when their independent bent seems to override their interdependent necessity for survival as a human order?

This observation of American society was ably documented by Alexis de Tocqueville in the early 1800s (1960 edition). He observed, "To the European, a public officer represents a superior force; to an American he represents a right. In America then, it may be said, that no one renders obedience to man, but to justice and to law. If the opinion that the citizen entertains of himself is exaggerated, it is at least salutary; he unhesitantly confides in his own power, which appears to him to be all-sufficient." The tendency of de Tocqueville to regard the concept of the citizens, not nations, as sovereign can only be truly understood in the context of the environment of American bureaucracy and community life (Emmerich 1978).

Contemporary Communities

Contemporary communities are complex, ever-changing social phenomena not insulated from the world beyond. They are multi-dimensional, territorial-oriented concepts of open social systems (Sanders 1972; Warren 1963, 1972; Hawley 1950). They can be viewed as an ecology, if you will, a holistic organization of social life and action. The main elements that have traditionally been used to describe communities are under attack because of difficulty in establishing or defining community boundaries, interactions, resources, and service. Today communities' organizational systems are influenced considerably by regional, national, and international activities. Today, no community is isolated or self-sufficient (Chekki 1990). Communities today are best described by Warren's (1972) notion of community in which units are parts of vertical and horizontal systems that people use to produce, distribute, and consume goods and services. Communities are dependent, interdependent, or independent of extra-community units and systems depending on the functions under analysis at a particular time and place. They are an ecology in which personality, organization, political power, interorganizational linkages, economic development, change, and innovation are but a few issues to be considered. Communities are ecological systems with inside and outside control points and at some times they are, in fact, uncontrollable systems.

Edwards and Jones (1976) believe that one has to know about community in order to effectively apply community development processes. They see community as a loosely based unit of social organization dependent on larger units of organizations found in society at large. Their conceptualizations of community include a measure or degree self-sufficiency as a functioning entity, but they acknowledge a community's interdependence among other community organizations and systems. For them, communities have group structure integrated around goals derived from members' collective life style and use of space.

Anthropological studies on the new international communities that form themselves within an increasingly anonymous larger society are reported by Misra and Preston (1978). Such communities are placed in a comparative framework of a worldwide array of other, longer-lasting societies. This is done by studying various styles of "communal living" in the USA, south Asia, former Soviet Union, and Israel. Misra and Preston's work sets the pattern for my view of communities as societies.

The Questioning Community

For Tinder (1980), communication is central to the idea of community. Communication is in the nature of inquiry concerned with truth, and is not passed by but transcends every explicit conclusion that emerges. Communities, as well as societies, cannot be sustained by simply transmitting what is securely known. It is essential to their survival that all knowledge is under constant questioning and reexamination.

Truth is what links human beings when they rise above confusion and dishonesty; in that way it is the substance of social life. Communities, as do societies, possess values in themselves, but also they test and enhance values of things that are shared. For Tinder, one has to make the assumption that community and society at large are tolerant especially of "irreverent questions" in order to understand or appreciate modern life.

Tinder (1980) believes that society is organized for action in hierarchies with inequalities of power, wealth, and control. Societies are moved by a logic of scale that is the larger, the stronger, the wealthier, etc. Communities within societies are governed by the principle of plurality; that is, no ideology or policy, no social entity, group, institution, or authority should be uncriticized. Each person should belong to several different groups, heed various authorities, and concede diverse social and political prescriptions.

The Community of Conflict

Political community denotes an association sustained by power from communities that we experience and the tensions that we accept as part of our humanity. For Tinder (1980), political community is where power is reliably subordinated to common inquiry. When a law is passed, the public inquires as to its common good. The cultural community comes into existence from public, scientific, historical, artistic, and philosophical inquiry. The cultural community value is its unconditional acceptance of all truths—the pure community. The private community is based on a right of exclusion or, in yet another view, as Schmitt and Weaver (1979) observe, community is where you find it. Thus community scholars must deal with many communities and numerous social systems and subsystems and their interrelationships. The idea of membership in several communities within and without a larger community is a powerful informal linking concept that contributes to our understanding of social networks called communities. These concepts are economic, residential, recreational, educational, political, religious, voluntary, etc., in which individuals have a choice to join and actively participate in for long-term as well as short-term or transitory periods of time. Ours is a community viewed as a system of social systems defined as a group of persons who are members of organized interest in which the action of one affects the action of others.

We see that a community must deal with relationships between groups. It is, in a sense, the moderator between differing parties in conflict. Communities provide a social guarantee of the rights and protections for groups and individuals alike (Scherer 1972). A community reflects many structured commonalities. A community has longevity, so—as with most modern social systems—it is difficult to determine where community begins and ends. The political aspects of community are pluralistic ideas related to structure, conflict, and power, all of which are interrelated. Conflict is necessarily of several types; it can be and, in many cases, is beneficial as well as harmful to communities and their members.

Planned Community Interaction

Modern communities are selected in large part by community members or by the voluntary involvement of individuals, probably based on the criterion of pleasure or satisfaction derived from participation. Many community programs directed at significant social change tend to fail due in large part to the inordinate complexity of planned intervention. Rothman et al. (1981) offers specific strategies or action guidelines to individuals, agencies, and organizations that engage in planned social change. Their suggestions or principles of community change and development intervention include the following:

* Promote an innovation by demonstrating it first with a small portion of the target population. Then expand it.

* Change an organization's goals by introducing a new group into the organization.

* Increase participation in organization and group activities by offering benefits for participation.

* Increase effectiveness by clarifying goals and obtaining agreement among relevant superiors and influentials.

Specific hypotheses for each of these general principles are presented for use by those of us who engage in community change efforts.

Schmitt and Weaver (1979) view community from the perspective of community educators and note that a sense of community includes at least the following points:

* An organizational structure through which collective action of two or more systems or subsystems is achieved

* The emergence of coordinating agencies to promote study of specific problems and coordinate that systems involvement to resolve the problem

* Opportunity for each individual to have membership and commitment to several communities

* Substantive involvement of citizens in all major agencies and institutions

* Evidence of the adoption of social norms and constraints appropriate to the area

* Commitment to lifelong learning with the realization of a society outside their private worlds

* Evidence of commitment to education

* Communication across system and subsystem boundaries or interaction between communities of interest

* Superordinate goals that are impossible to reach without obtaining cooperation across social system boundaries

* Evidence of accommodation and mediation within and across diverse and sometimes conflicting social systems

* Access to information required to resolve social and environmental problems

* Access to state, national, and global systems through which to solve problems inside as well as outside the area

This is a list I find most useful for anyone interested in understanding or activating community change. It goes beyond most traditional thinking and includes concepts like lifelong education, communication, mediation, and linkage of networks. From my experience, I would add the importance of factoring in transportation and telecommunication as necessary aspects of any concept of community.

The "information society" is upon us (Lundstedt 1990). Telecommunication technology has literally exploded over the past 10 to 15 years and accelerated our dependence upon ready access and availability of information. This fact raises the question: Is telecommunication technology forcing a fundamental redefinition of values in our society? And the answer has to be an emphatic yes. For example, through telecommunication we now carry out commercial transactions, shop at home, transfer large amounts of information across long distances and international boundaries, have access to other personal and corporate records at our finger tips. All of these and more form our public opinion, politics, and generally affect all our space and behavior.

Our values of economics, social, psychological, political exchange, and privacy are directly affected by this high technology, but how and to what end? Certainly telecommunication technology and values are interrelated. Such values are defined as an element of a person's feelings and a coherent system of beliefs as reflected in their culture. Information is, in fact, power which is used and does affect our lives for good and for bad.

Community as a Social System

Warren (1972) sets the stage for our conceptualization of a community as a social system. A social system is a structural organization of interaction of units which endure through time. As such the community has both external and internal relationships to its units as well as to its environment. The community separates itself from its environment by a process called boundary maintenance which helps maintain it in equilibrium in the larger ever changing system in which it exists.

I, as does Warren (1972), at this point present some definitions of terms to be used in our treatment of the interorganizational community.

Community: The organization of social activities to afford people daily local access to those broad areas of activity necessary in daily living. That combination of social units and systems which perform the major social functions having locality relevance.

Community
functions: The local participation and access to the process of production, distribution and consuming goods and services which are part of daily living

The process by which society or one of its constituent social units transmits prevailing knowledge, social values, and behavior pattern to its individual members

The process through which a group influences the behavior of its members toward conformity with its norms

The process of providing individuals local access to its basic units of organizations

The process of providing individuals local support and care in the time of sickness, of economic distress and other welfare concerns

The process whereby the identity of a social system is preserved and the characteristic interacting pattern of the system is preserved and maintained

These concepts denote a communities' capacity to satisfy a human desire which is attributed to any object, idea, or content of experience. They are the underlying principles according to which people and their organizations make choices.

Chapter 2

THE SOCIETY

Community and the trials it imposes on human beings in history are not readily understood through systematic theories. Systematic political theory often useful, always falsifies since reality itself is not systematic. The lack of systematic unity does not imply a lack of substantial unity (Tinder 1980, 11).

In an effort to better understand community, despite our inability to do so through systematic theories, we will back up and see if clarity is possible through a review of social theory and societal perspectives. Society in Aristotle's terms means men joining together merely for the sake of life, i.e., survival; the good life comes later. For Aristotle the roots of society are physical, spiritual, and social necessities of human survival.

Structural Theories

Levy (1966), in her effort to understand society in the modern world, has identified elements of behavior common to all societies. For her the following aspects of behavior are present in all societies:

*   Role definition
*   Solidarity
*   Economic allocation
*   Political allocation
*   Integration and expression including socialization, religion, education, and recreation

She argues that if the society is at all stable, these aspects of behavior are always highly structured, never random or chaotic.   According to Levy (1966), the common organizations of societies are:

The family	Family is the surest and most fundamental community organization. The family is a major focus of social behavior. The role of the individual in the family is always relevant ideally and/or actually in all other organizations distinguished by members of the society.
Government	Government is always present in any society of scale. Government always involves a combination of centrality and decentralization and particularistic selection.
Economic sets	Economic sets are organizations that provide for exchange of goods and services. Some of these sets are also considered to be socially illegitimate and a major factor for graft and corruption within a society. Economic sets never exist unless there is a government in the society.
Other organizations	Society is composed of formal and informal units organized on a predominately particularistic basis such as armed forces, schools, churches, etc. When

other organizations emerge, economic sets, government, and family organizations are always present.
This fact causes problems of interrelationships
between the members of all societies' organizational
types. Government and family are the most important to social life, but no organized society can
afford to ignore problems associated with its
economic systems or its other organizations.

Within this framework of society, according to Levy (1966), there
are some common relationships that always emerge. The first is the
problem of tradition, in the underlying set of relationships that emerge
for all organizations. Then there is the common set of specialized
relationships associated with society's member contacts with strangers,
and members' emphasis on rationality, universalism, functional
specificity, and avoidance. Finally, there are some common problems of
socialization, economic allocation, political stability, and discrepancies
between ideal and actual structures that.are present in all societal
organizations.

Mysior (1977) argues that we tend to see trees not forests. We
as scholars give up on the whole or complexity of social systems in favor
of abstractions and social fragmentation. Society is seen as a system
under constant change and self-correcting conditions that are designed
to remain within tolerant limits for that society. Mysior notes that there
seems to be an interdependence of all social variables relating back to
the prevalent paradigms or conceptualizations of the phenomenon at the
time. For him, a system is any aggregate of parts that are interrelated
in an organized way. The relationship between the parts is seen as

functional or dependent on the action of another part. The elements of these parts exhibit variables of different values or magnitude within the system. Under this scheme, boundaries of a system are like a puzzle, not self-evident, and ever changing, but they become established through successively more precise definition, perception of more environmental constraints, and a resulting modification of boundaries to accommodate such forces. As Warren (1972) has noted, community system boundaries are both geographic and psychological. People, after all, are the members of social systems and as such their belonging— who is in and who is out—may be as difficult to determine as is the physical shifting geographic boundary, but both in fact do exist.

Theory of Structuration

The post-empiricism theory of structuration is a social theory recently put forward by Gidden. While not universally convincing, it is viewed by many modern scholars as one of the most systematic and sustained social theory known (Bryant and Jary 1991).

Gidden has attempted to determine the conditions which govern the continuity and dissolution of structures in society. For him, structuration is the dynamic process whereby structures come into being, become productive, and reproduce. It differs from structuralism where the reproduction of social relations and practice are viewed simply as a mechanical outcome; structuralism is sometimes called the philosophy of action. It is a philosophy that attempts to show how social structures are constituted by human agency, and yet Gidden points out that social structures are the very medium of this constitution. Gidden argues this is a dualism of agency and structure in social action, which is not very useful when attempting to explain and understand society. Gidden attempts to avoid this dualism by separating the system and the structure and then tries to explain how social practice came about. He notes that structures are constituted through action and, reciprocally, that action is constituted structurally. Gidden does not refer to the descriptive analysis of interaction relationship which compares organizations or collectives (functionalism), but he refers to systems of generative rules and resources that members draw upon and change in the continuous production and reproduction of organizations in society. For him, social systems are equal to the surface patterns of interaction structures that compose the virtual order of generative rules and resources.

For Gidden, homeostatic feedback loops are causal factors that play an important but largely unintended feedback on system reproduction in traditional structural-functional theories. In his structuration theory, these homeostatic loops play an important integral and expected part in the reproduction of social systems. For Gidden, intended self-regulation and reflexive self-regulation are causal loops in which the feedback is affected by at least three levels of an actor's knowledge or consciousness of the action that is occurring. He illustrates his stratification model of action by noting these three layers of consciousness:

* Reflexive monitoring of action and discursive consciousness based on what actors are able to say about the conditions of their own actions.

*   Rationalization of action and practical consciousness based
        on what actors know but cannot articulate about their own
        actions.

*   Unconscious motives, i.e., cognitions that are repressed by
        the actors. They are semiotic impulses, affecting motiva-
        tion but barred from the actor's consciousness.

All three levels of actions and consciousness are potentially
implicated in the production and reproduction of social systems. This is
true for Gidden despite the existence of unacknowledged conditions and
unintended consequences of any model that purports to explain social
systems.

Gidden argues that any theory that seeks to explain social systems
in terms of unintended reproduction is unbalanced. In other words he
believes the unintended must be expected and is dealt with by the
system. His theory argues that all processes of the structuration of
systems of social interaction involve the elements of:

*   The communication of meaning
*   The exercise of power
*   The evaluation and judgment of conduct

Time and space relation are core to Gidden's theory. Structures
are immersed in social interactions and systems which are located in,
and shaped by, time and space. Environmental relations external to
social relations shape the social content of time and space so as to make
them internal to social relations. Both the reversible and irreversible time
of day-to-day experiences of institutions, as well as the irreversible time
of the life course, structure social relations across time and space.

Bryant and Jary (1991) offer in Figure 1 a comparison between key concepts of Gidden's structuration theory and the more traditional functionalism theory of society.

FUNCTIONALISM
Basic concepts

(a) System interdependence of action, conceived of only as homeostatic causal loops

(b) Structure—stable pattern of action

(c) Functions and dysfunctions— contribution of system 'parts' to whole in promoting system integration or disintegration

(d) Manifest and latent functions— intended (anticipated) contributions and unintended (unanticipated) contributions to system integration

STRUCTURATION THEORY
Basic concepts

(a) System interdependence of action, conceived of as:
  (i) homeostatic causal loops
  (ii) self-regulation via feedback
  (iii) reflexive self-regulation

(b) Structure—generative rules and resources

(c) Structuration—generation of systems of interaction through duality of structure

(d) Production and reproduction society—accomplishment of interaction under bounded conditions of rationalization of action, i.e., actors produce social action (as a 'skilled performance') but do so in situations in which there are also 'unacknowledged conditions'

Figure 1.   ***Key concepts of structuration theory and functionalism compared***
Source: Adapted from Gidden 1977a; Bryant and Jary 1991.

My understanding of social order, like Gidden's, draws heavily on social phenomenology and ethnomethodology. I believe the world is

known to us as members of the social order by our perceptions of the
order of things. In a real sense our conscious as well as our
unconscious — mostly linguistic — notions or conceptions of structure and
the rules of structure govern our behavior in relation to and within the
world we live in. All types of rules, moral and other, that emerge seem
to be interpretive schemes that make sense of what actors say and do,
as well as all cultural objects they produce. Finally, for Gidden, power
is defined as the transformative capacity actors have as they apply
resources (material and nonmaterial) to given situations in the facility or
their structures using all known or generative rules that are appropriate
to the situation.

Theories of Fragmentation of Consciousness

Tinder (1980), commenting on the nature of community, argues
that humans are 'inquirers' who transcend every social role by continual
questioning and criticizing of everything they experience. This phenomenon has the effect of disrupting or deunifying the community. Tinder
accounts for this by his theory of fragmentation of consciousness. For
him there are four models of consciousness. The first two are experience and awareness, which are cognitive; the other two are represented
by the artist and the saint and are called vision and faith. The social
philosopher Mead (1934; Aboulafia 1991) deals with the phenomenon
of cognition consciousness in his treatment of self in specific social
roles. Mead believed, as do many, that the organized society, or the
community of social groups, gives to an individual a unity of self called

the "generalized other." For Mead, the attitude of the generalized other is reflective of and is, in fact, the attitude of the whole community.

For some scholars, inquiry is the effort to elucidate and to harmonize the modes of consciousness. We do this by the scientific ordering of things into forms of expression or the historical recording of the persons, places, and events that are not reducible to universals, plus the ordered things that are. We also rely on transcendental queries based on vision and faith. Finally, our appeal is to the philosophical, which is empty in form but brings the unique function of reason and thought to the process.

The Metronomic Society

Young (1988) in his book talks about the phenomena of the *cyclical*, which keeps things the same by reproducing the past, and the *lineal*, which makes things different by introducing novelty and creating the new dimensions of society. These two dimensions of time are necessary to human life and are dependent upon each other. They may be viewed as two ways, not always complementary, of looking at the same thing. They are only views at different moments of time. Young argues that neither the future nor the past exists in reality, only the present, and only the memories of past things form our understanding of present things and direct our perceptions of future things. For Young, expectations exist in the human mind but nowhere else.

Continuities of life are preserved and reproduced by cyclical change such as language or culture as a whole. Discontinuities are lineal changes that never return or recycle. Young's thesis is that the cyclical change accounts for how society maintains continuity, and it is the essence of social science. Society also has a lineal basis that adds social rhythms and change to it.

Society means nothing unless it possesses a measure of stability over time. Some elements must have continuity and reproduceability and not be left only to history but as Young, Tinder, Gidden, and I argue, these elements must exist with a dynamic concept of recognizable change. This view of society is not as static as is much of traditional sociology of the past. It is a view of social structures, from ancient Maya to modern Japanese, in which life is made up of cyclical or reproductive changes rather than static changes, and where expected lineal changes of life replace the concept of the unintended. We see society with a structure not fixed like a stone but more like a bubble tent, which is ever-changing.

Young sees the world, as do I, as an array of interlocking or interflowing cycles with their own spheres of partial independence. There are daily cycles, wake-sleep cycles, lunar cycles, annual cycles, stimulus-response cycles, clocks, schools, sport, academic calendars, habits, customs, etc. These cycles can be likened to fly wheels. If you will, fly wheels of society which invoke authority, and while authority bolsters custom, custom also bolsters authority habits which are exhibited in all societies.

In both cultural and genetic systems nearly all changes occur at the margin, that is, building incrementally on what is already there. In society, every proposal for an innovation in behavior must compete with many other proposals, most of which are discarded, but also has to be compatible with previous behavior. To be adopted, an idea has to gain acceptance by being kneaded in with what is already there, capturing for the new idea some legitimacy formally attached to the old way of behaving.

Young (1988) notes that in law the most vital element is precedent, which attaches authority to repetition of an idea, but lawyers are proud of their capacity for blending innovation with precedent. They constantly challenge and try to change old precedents and form new precedents. This change in precedent impels legal forces forward to the future. This notion of law represents a good model of how, always building on tradition, substantiated change is brought about in society. Customs and beliefs establish a rule or formula for social behavior. Over time, customs and beliefs change, but the rule remains. New beliefs are used to account for the rule and to reconcile it with the present state of things, thus adapting the rule to a new form that then governs social behavior.

The Cooperative Value Process

Young (1988) views society as the most spectacular cooperative in existence. Cooperation has over time steadily extended the habit of mind, and the stores of information shared by many people in many societies worldwide. We have ideas that we think are our own but are really the cooperative idea of many others. Without this principle of cooperation—sociability and material aid—human society could not ameliorate its environment so as to function and survive. Our mutual dependence, adult to adult, children to adults, adult to organization, organization to organization, has led to this social evolution called civilization.

Dirrell (1936), in a philosophical work exploring the general scientific principles of cooperation, noted that every act of cooperation involves the following elements:

*   Individualism that is the utmost development of each unit in the cooperating group, the persons, the ideas, or the objects.

*   Altruism which is the radiation from each unit of the utmost help or value to all.

*   Balance of life itself: I, you, we. Here positives are more important than negatives.

*   Inner considerations that are more important than outer considerations.

Dirrell views cooperation as both a science and an art, a science of teamwork involving materials, form, and uses that act to balance individual interests with those of the group. Cooperation is more difficult when it involves personal rather than impersonal values. Loose forms of cooperation tend to yield much greater multiplication of value and general higher aggregates of personal joy than close or tight forms. So in every person's life, no matter how closely they cooperate with some groups, it is important to have a reserve, dignity, or independence in order to achieve personal joy and peace. It is this blend of independence and dependence that enables us to reach the highest development possible. The balance between I-ism, you-ism, and we-ism, is essential. This form of cooperation puts cultural and ideal values in first place, with money and material values second and auxiliary.

For Dirrell, two philosophies of life are important:

*   That which lays primary emphasis on the unit.

*   That which pays leading attention to the multiplier.

Such cooperation occurs when the unit equals people, money, material possessions, etc., and the multiplier equals value orders placed on units, and when use is that which enhances the effects and values to self or others. This is the type of higher multiplier effect which is worth more than mere acquisition. When the principle of unit exploitation on behalf of self and others takes place in geometrical progressions, it will always be of major importance to humans who balance cooperative effort with self and other interest.

To what end then should we cooperate? For what good? For what purpose? For what good life?

*   Epicureanism or hedonism which seeks the pleasures of life.

*   Utilitarianism that provides the greatest good for the greatest number of people.

*   Pragmatism where the primary category is value and secondary are reality and cognitions.

Dirrell believes that values should be explored and exploited vigorously. He calls this the value process philosophy. He freely pursues any good end or value that appears with the utmost expansion and aggressiveness. It is this type of aggressiveness that causes individuals to cooperate and thus develop a higher human value. With this value process, both magic (art) and the machine (science) are followed but magic dominates.

Recently Deutsch (1990) reported on a series of experiments focused on the conditions under which people cooperate. Researchers asked, under what conditions are people with conflicting interests able to work out an agreement, or a system of justice that defines what each shall give and receive in the transaction between them, that is stable and mutually satisfying? They found that cooperative systems of interaction that were experienced as fair by participants foster the development and maintenance of that system. The opposite was true of competitive type system of cooperation and researchers also found that perceived fair agreements are enhanced when conflicting parties have a positive interest in each other.

Deutsch (1990) also reported on experiments dealing with the effects of different systems of distributive justice. Such studies offered little support for the equity theory. Subjects were motivated to perform well more because of their own need to do so than because they might receive a greater amount of pay, or because of the actor's good performance, or when the winner takes all, or when pay was proportional to the actor's contribution. In other words, good performance was determined more by self-imposed standards than by external rewards. External factors seemed only to come into play when participants were alienated from their work or participation. However, distributive systems of justice in which the group functions are important significantly affect members' social attitudes and the social relations that develop within the group. External factors tend to enhance a member's performance but tend to diminish such performance if the cooperating group demands actions that are incongruent with the established social relations in that distributive system.

Chapter 3

THE ORGANIZATION

Complex societies are just that—complex, and cannot be understood in the simpler communities of the past. Bureaucracies are the most central, ubiquitous, and powerful elements of complex society (Britan and Cohen 1980).

In my search for understanding of community I have reviewed classic community theory as well as generally acknowledged societal theory. I do, in fact, find useful explanations in both, but also end up with a feeling of incompleteness and inadequacy in my search for perceptions and descriptions of the communities I have experienced. This is not a feeling of hopelessness or unhappiness with the work of thinkers past and present; rather, it's a confirmation of my humanity. To be human is to be incapable of comprehending the whole. We survive this limitation by abstracting various properties of the phenomena that interest us. Out of these abstractions or perceptions we form images in our consciousness—and, for that matter, unconsciousness—that mean something to us and govern our behavior in relation to those experiences. It is with that understanding of my human limitations that I continue to draw on the abstractions and perceptions of others that account for or explain some aspect of life, even if these explanations are contradictory, ambiguous, nonlogical, nonrational, or nonsensical when viewed in relationship to each other. I am comfortable and can move forward with my current understanding of the issues.

As does Presthus (1978), I view organizations as miniature societies in which the dominant values of society are inculcated and sought and accommodated by individual organizational members. Contemporary organizations have a pervasive influence upon individual and group behavior. Organizations define permanent social systems that are designed to achieve limited objectives through their members. All organizations in which people spend their working lives have critical normative consequences as they provide the environment in which most of our lives are spent. They are the major disciplinary force of our society, and our economic, spiritual, and intellectual worlds. The accepted values of organizations shape individuals' personalities and behavior. As such, organizations shape and define human worth, dignity, and the capacity to reason and discover. Our acceptance of this organizational life sets the emergence of the bureaucratic model as the major organizational form in our society. This is true in virtually every social area. Individuals are conditioned to accept and participate in the legitimacy of authority, division of labor, and differentiation, and conditional participation of organized behavior.

Along with Presthus, I argue that bureaucratic organizations provide a structured field in which the symbols of authority, status, and functional roles tend to be exceptionally significant and compelling. Therefore we should work hard to understand, and then improve, organizations and the existing systems, in so doing we will improve the human condition and reduce the tragic waste of human talent and individual creativity that some scholars ascribe to organizational life.

Social Rule Systems Theory

Burns and Flam (1987) believe that social rule system theory can be used to describe and explain the formation and reformation of major types of social organization in contemporary society. In organization coalitions such as government, planning systems, interorganizational networks, markets, negotiation systems, and work organizations, members (individuals, groups, organization, communities, and other collectivities) produce and live by social rule systems that structure and regulate all transactions for all organizations. Coalition organizations are linked to conflicts and struggles about establishing consensus and showing social actors how to knowingly and actively use, interpret, and implement such rule systems. Organizational members or actors in the end create, reform, and transform rules to bring about innovation and shape complex organizational networks and systems that structure human history.

A community or society consists of a human population that shares abstract as well as detailed knowledge of major social rules systems. The theory deals with power and knowledge, that is, the activation of power to set rules and the application of knowledge to formulate and interpret rules. Rule systems are found in all social groups, organizations, communities, and societies in three main institutionalized forms (Burns and Flam 1987):

* Hierarchial forms, which are the rational-legal organizations that authorize and legitimize judicial and administrative systems.

* Democratic forms such as election procedure in which both public and private spheres of organization, associations, parties, community groups operate by some type of vote system.

* Negotiative or contractual forms involving social networks that may be interorganizational, intercorporate and international in scale.

There is a "rule system" dominance of some system or systems over others, but this dominance is rarely total. In most cases all forms of rule systems are employed. For most issues participating agents are able to introduce illegitimate or unofficial rule systems so that no one organization, community, or nation will gain and hold control over time.

Boundaries of Organizational Systems

Haas and Drabek (1973) view organizations as complex, relatively permanent, interaction systems. Their boundaries as defined are highly dependent on the specific interest of the investigator or by what gives meaning to the observer. Boundaries of an interacting system can be identified based on the frequency and the content of interactions, the pattern of interactions, and the recurrence of patterns. An important factor to drawing such boundaries is where the interaction occur. Organizational boundaries are established in an environment that forms a relationship of high interdependence between the organization and the setting in which it interacts. It is the environment that defines the limits of the external constraint structure. The environment's impact on the units is not uniform throughout; rather, it varies depending on time, stability, and location. Members' interactions are also variables upon which observers tend to draw boundaries for organizations and their interacting systems. Two criteria seem to be most significant: the frequency of interaction and the content of interaction.

Note of Concern

Schwartz (1990) along with many other scholars, is distressed to find most theories in the area of organization are almost always found to be useless when organizational reality more closely approximates a snake pit rather than the bland, ordered, and productive picture much organizational theory conveys. Given this predisposition, Schwartz observes that antisocial actions seem to be built into the process of organizational socialization on how organizations deal with favorable as well as unfavorable environments. He believes that as organizations face disfavor or degeneration in society, they frequently require their members to engage in deviant or antisocial behavior for the good of the organization. Such organizational tolitarianism tends to place falsehood at the core of organizational functioning. This leads to an acceleration of the organization's decay and demise as well as much antisocial behavior on the part of its members. Even in light of this phenomenon, Schwartz is optimistic that society recognizes this addictive type of built-in antisocial organizational socialization pattern, and treats it as an organizational addiction that can be corrected when recognized.

Perceptual Theory and Organization

An organization is only something in the minds of people—it is an image. An image may be defined as an alterable state of knowledge which governs behavior (Boulding 1961):

* It is only what is believed by the possessor to be true.

* It is a result of all past experiences of its possessor.

* It is the everyday situation of self and surroundings taken to be reality.

* It has no necessary connection with good or bad, accurate or inaccurate, adequate or inadequate of the possessor's judgment.

* It is reality to possessors and as such it governs their behavior. At any instance, the possessor's behavior is purposeful, relevant, and pertinent to the situation as the possessor understands it.

The notion that an organization is nothing more or less than an image suggests that use of perceptual theory to analyze organizational behavior is appropriate. The phenomenological approach to the study of organizational behavior is concerned with the observation of behavior through the senses, that is, sensed or reported by that which is behaving or experiencing. This is an internal rather than an external approach to the study of organization behavior.

The analyst attempts to view the situation from the point of view of the specific organization and its members in order to predict what that organization will do in another given situation.

Example: Part of our perceived social reality of organization is the definition of behavior expectations we hold on at least three levels of perception, i.e., perceived expectations, as —

* A position incumbent of an organization.

* A subpart or division of an organization.

* A specific organization in relationship to the larger society of which it is a part.

What Is an Organization?

An organization is a system of consciously coordinated personal activities or forces of two or more people. It is a problem-solving mechanism that depends on factoring general goals into subgoals.

An organization comes into being when —

* there are persons able to communicate with each other

* who are willing to contribute action

* to accomplish a common purpose

Cooperation occurs only when individual limitations become significant factors in goal achievement and when the application of the energy of two or more people will overcome this individual limitation. A person must be induced to cooperate or there can be no cooperation. The net satisfactions that induce a person to contribute effort to an organization result from that person's assessment of the advantages and disadvantages of the cooperation.

Specialization is an organizational phenomenon; it is the product of analysis of purpose within an organization, and is what adds power to cooperative efforts. Specialization is reflected in a division of labor, which is an essential aspect of any organization. Specialization of tasks within an organization:

*   Is a result of technological development as such old specialties are replaced by new specialties.

*   Is dependent upon activities and processes beyond the control of the organization, making the organization dependent upon other activities going on in society.

*   Tends to create organizational interdependence as reflected in the relationship between ability, influence, and authority of possessing members within an organization.

*   Should be initiated based on advances in specific specializations and not simply on the acts of organizational authority.

Organizational cooperation under advanced specialization depends upon recognized and accepted mutual interdependence of subparts of the total organized system.

Organization as a Social System

An organization as a social system is a collection of people drawn together as a body born to achieve a common goal or goals. In other words, an organization is a group of individuals working together in a structured manner and dedicated to achieve specific, defined goals.

Barnard (1938), in his book *The Function of the Executive*, has described an organization as a system of cooperative human activities, the functions of which are creation, transformation, and exchange of utilities. As a social system, an organization exhibits certain patterns of behavior and interaction that are observable and predictable. As a social system, an organization exhibits the following characteristics; Loomis (1960) calls these conditions of social action:

*   Unity or cohesion
*   Boundaries
*   Resistance to external forces
*   Continuity through time
*   Location in space
*   Facilities to achieve goals

As a social system, an organization is composed of the following elements:

*   **Beliefs**—any proposition about any aspect of the universe that is accepted as true.

*   **Sentiments**—primary expressions that represent what actors feel about the world no matter why they feel it.

*   **Goals**—the ends toward which behavior is directed.

*   **Norms**—standards of expected and prescribed ways for actors to behave in relation to the organizations goals; "rules of the game," written and unwritten.

*   **Position**—roles of the behavior expected of members in any given situation.

*   **Status**—the ordering or. ranking of actors; that may be either ascribed or achieved.

*   **Power**—the influence, the authority, the ability or the right to influence and control the behavior of actors. Authority and influence both must be present for the development of power.

> * Sanctions—the patterns of rewards and punishments meted out by the actors of the system which encourage behavior that conforms to the norms established to achieve the organization's goals.

As a social system, an organization utilizes the following processes to mesh, stabilize, and alter relationships between the elements through time. These processes give the system a dynamic functioning continuity.

> * **Communications** is the process by which information, decisions, and directives are transmitted among actors and the ways in which knowledge, opinions, and attitudes are formed or modified by interaction.

> * **Socialization** is the process through which the social and cultural heritage is transmitted.

> * **Problem solving,** including **decision making,** is the process of reaching a conclusion on an issue under consideration.

> * **Boundary maintenance** is the process whereby the identity of the social system is preserved and the characteristic interaction pattern maintained.

> * **Systems linkage** is the process whereby one or more of the elements of at least two social systems is articulated in such a manner that in some way and some occasions they may be viewed as a single unit.

> * **Evaluation** is the process of fixing the value or worth of any object or activity.

> * **Social control** is the process by which deviancy is either eliminated or somehow made compatible with the function of the social groups.

Organization as a System of Planned Change

If we think of an organization as a type of a factory, we see that raw resources of various kinds (inputs) are drawn together at the factory. These resources are combined in the factory and, in the process, a new product of use is formed. Likewise, inputs of resources through an organization may result in the production of a new product, a product that could not have been achieved without the use of organizational effort.

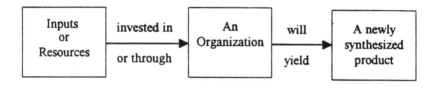

Figure 2:   *Input-output model of organization action*

We now can see that an organization can be a useful tool with which to transform raw resources of given types into the planned production of a desirable change or product. This planned change could not have been accomplished as easily without organizational action. In general, the outcomes of organized action are more controllable and predictable than are the outcomes of individual actions.

Social Power and the Demand for Its Control

All systems that deal with or attempt to explain human behavior ultimately get involved with control or mastery of material and nonmaterial resources. Control is a nasty word to many people. We say we don't want to be controlled. However, history records the human-kind's extensive efforts to control all that it experiences. Power is the ability to motivate people to move or act in a predictable direction or manner.

* Naturalists view control as a natural phenomenon and believe that people had no control of, or effect on, nature.

* Darwinists take the view that humans have some control over their environment.

* Economists see human beings as rational beings who have even greater control of their environment and who could make decisions from alternatives.

* Freudians approach controls as a phenomenon arising from the self and from the self in relationship to others.

* Sociologists attempt to deal with control and power in terms of social role theory within organizations, which includes—

   * Basic personality patterns.

   * Normative behavior of living by the rules of our own given society and its network of relationships.

   * These norms or rules of life then are detailed and specific, which produce reliable desired behavior patterns.

One of humankind's most pronounced characteristics is our search and effort to control everything that exists. What we see, what we can reach, we manipulate and deal with as we come in contact with it. Margaret Mead calls attention to the fact that the development of human society on a large scale has led to almost complete control by people.

People establish their own home where they wish; build cities around their homes; bring water and other necessities great distances; establish the vegetation that will grow; determine the animals that will exist; determine which insects shall continue to live; determine which micro organisms shall remain in the environment. People determine, by means of clothing and housing, what temperatures shall be. We regulate the extent of our environment by our methods of locomotion. The whole onward struggle of humankind's existence on the face of the earth is a determination of what life shall exist about us and, as such, our control of objects that determine and affect our very own life. People thus create and modify their environment by being sensitive to it.

Social control, viewed as a constructive force in human society, has a built-in form of self-evaluation, in that individuals can compare their actions and philosophy against the norms, rules, and regulations established and enforced by the society. Social control does not tend to crush the individual or obliterate self-conscious individuality. On the contrary, social control is actually constructive and inextricably associated with individuality, for the individual is a conscience personality only to the extent that he or she is a member of society and involved in the social processes of experience and activity. This activity, to be purposeful and meaningful, must be controlled.

People, in their effort to meet their need for control, invented the organization. Many people today react negatively to organizations and their conglomerated bureaucracies. One bad experience with an organization often creates for an individual a reality in which all organizations are rigid, impersonal, undemocratic, and to be avoided if possible. But organizations serve as mechanisms for extending human capacities to achieve reliability of human behavior over time and, in so doing, facilitate the achievement of desired goals or anticipated consequences. This tool, however, is not perfect; almost every recorded effort to organize has produced undesired or unanticipated consequences because almost all activities in these organizations are based on imperfect knowledge. This general phenomenon is illustrated in Figure 3.

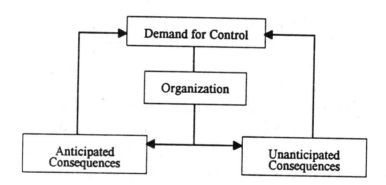

Figure 3: *Demand for control - a general model*

Application of the model depends largely on the role prescribed by the organization for the individual. Equally important is the role expectation perceived and defined by each individual. Organizational members' behavior expectations are conditioned by society's expectations. The model starts with organizational control strategies as the independent variable, with anticipated and unanticipated consequences as the dependent variables. The consequence is registered in terms of causal feedback loops of anticipated consequences that tend to reinforce and stabilize the mode of organization. Both the rule making and delegation approaches have dysfunctional consequences for an organization which tend to intensify its need for control. This process is summarized in the following demand-for-control model in Figure 4.

Organization Life Cycle

The birth and death of organizations is a fascinating concept documented by many scholars (Kimberly et al. 1980). The abbreviated version below is one I find most useful because it focuses on how an organization shifts its allocation of resources over its life span.

Birth Period

The birth of an organization is seldom a spectacular overnight success. Rather, this is the time when a particular good or service is needed, one that for one reason or another is not generally accessible or available. The organization is formed in an attempt to satisfy the need. This period is usually marked by:

> * A sharp differentiation of the organization's values, purposes, and goals.

> * A type of dedicated "pioneering" in such goal product efforts as—

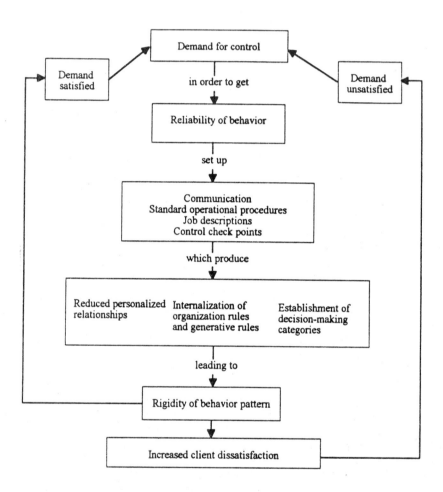

Figure 4: *Organizational demand for control model*

       *   Securing support for continual operations

       *   Developing the manner for product production

       *   Securing the acceptance of product utility in a general monopolistic market situation

* Of the total organizational resources available, a large proportion will be invested in maintenance, promotion, and goal product design and development activities.

* This is normally an unprofitable phase of operation and requires a futures type of expectation financing.

Growth Period

By now the organization is beginning to take a stable form. The goals product of the organization have met initial tests of utility. Demand for the goal product is rising at an accelerated rate. An environmental symptom of organizational success is the emergence of similar but competitive organizations. This period is usually marked by:

* Crystallization of organization values, purposes, and goals begins to occur.

* A type of dedicated "production" era in goal product achievement:

       *   Input resources for continuous operations are assured.

       *   Organizational products are accepted and demanded.

* Innovative goal product improvements are made in an effort to gain an advantage over the competitors product in a growing competitive market situation.

* In the allocation of the total resources, there are heavy investments in organizational product production and distribution with proportionally little emphasis or investments to maintain or justify organizational goal efforts.

* This is a period of goal product profitability for the organization, especially for the early innovating organization.

Maturity Period

Not only has the organization established a highly standardized rigid mode of operation, so have most of its competitors. Organizational innovation has now been replaced by the tendency to copy competing product features. This period is marked by:

* Organizational values, purposes, and goals that are difficult to differentiate from the many competing organizations.

* An economizing type of mass production era in goal product achievement.

* Input resources for continuous operations are more difficult to secure.

* Production problems have been worked out, operating procedures highly standardized, and product variety and variability markedly reduced.

* Heavy market competition for a highly standardized product offers the product user a wide range of product sources.

* A sharp reduction in the total resource investments in goods or product production accompanied by a proportional increase in maintenance-type promotional goal product justification investment. The organization now appeals to emotional/psychological factors and attributes of the organization and goal products rather than product utility and quality factors.

* The profits to the organization decline during this period. Maintenance costs rise, promotional and justifications costs rise, product production costs decline, product price is cut in an attempt to gain a larger share of the market. Organizations producing inferior products are generally forced off the market during this highly competitive period.

Decline and Death Period

The decline of an organization is seldom spectacular or an overnight event. Rather, it is the time when the market for a particular good or service reaches and extends beyond the saturation point. It is the period when an organization's primary goal becomes one of justifying its existence. The period is generally marked by:

* The complete rigidification of values, purposes, and goals. Innovation rarely, if ever, occurs at this stage.

* A type of dedicated justification in such goal efforts is developed based largely on the past accomplishments and utility of the organization and its products.

*   Input resources for continued operation are generally
       not forthcoming. Rather, the organization survives
       on past obligations and nondepreciated assets of the
       firm.

*   The goal product is produced primarily for those
       users who are still satisfied with the older product.
       Emphasis is again placed on product price, quality,
       and service.

*   Profits, while declining, may be maintained by
       efficient organizations that now, as they did in the
       beginning, tend to re-experience a monopolistic
       competitive situation. Product users now must again
       rely on the organization for their needed products
       and services.

*   This period is marked by promotional messages
       aimed at reminding product users of the great service
       the organization has provided to them throughout the
       years. Little or no new investment occurs. Of the
       total resource base, maintenance expenditures are
       proportionately high but are minimized wherever
       possible. Operations are generally geared to utiliza-
       tion of undepreciated assets of the organization.

*   As competitors drop out of the market place,
       efficient organizations maintain profits at a declining
       rate for an extended period. Eventually product sales
       decline which, coupled with a depleted asset base,
       forces the organization to cease operation.

Entrepreneurial and Innovative Spirit for the Future

Bratkovich et al. (1989) note that many business organizations
emerged from the 1980s with their competitive environment greatly
changed. More aggressive global technology seems to have eroded their

competitive advantage. What used to be winning strategies for the organization in the past are now very ineffective. A common organization theme heard today is the call to increase innovation by revitalizing entrepreneurial spirit within the organization. This call is in stark contrast to historical practice in which internal organizational contest tended to render efforts to maintain internal innovative units within the organization fruitless. Bratkovich et al. argue that venture teams can succeed if structure, staffing, and management are committed to innovation and, more importantly, if the reward system of the organization is geared for innovative efforts. Their idea is still a controversial element of internal management, but researchers cited case studies to show how this has been done by using strategies of subordination, decentralization, down-sizing the organization, and use of special rewards for acceptance of innovations. Basically there has to be a strategy to create and maintain an entrepreneurial subculture where innovations can flourish within the parent organization's environment. This is generally done by allowing for higher risk-taking, longer term horizons, and the design of rewards that recognize innovative work.

Holt (1989) claims that organizational survival in the 1990s and through the 21st century requires that organizations create and sustain cultures that encourage and nurture innovation and entrepreneurial spirit. She notes also that in our historic past most of such efforts have failed because organizations as systems tend to isolate and limit change from within and maintain status quo conditions. Holt uses Union Carbide as a case to illustrate how an old firm can establish an enabling environment that supports internal innovative success.

Niehaus and Price (1989) note there is a direct relationship between strategic direction or vision of an organization and the culture which must carry it out. To that end most studies about the successful use of research and development or other such innovative structures conclude that such ventures must be protected from the rest of the organization by someone at the top in high authority.

Innovation in organizational life was recently the topic of European scholars (Ciciotti and Thwaites 1990). Technological change and local economic development were analyzed from a variety of national and international contexts. Ciciotti and Thwaites made a functional analysis of sets of components that make up larger markets in relation to future development of technology maintained through organizations with rigid ties between the company and the outside world. They studied innovation, diffusion and adoption of products and technology, and they examined worldwide structures or systems within systems, from a local plant to a city, state, and nation. Ciotti and Thwaites found in all these studies that while there is a strong desire for organizations to be independent and monopolistic, the reality of their dependence and control by forces outside their own environment is absolute.

Chapter 4

THE ENVIRONMENT

Ecology theories deal with the adjustment of human beings to their environment, and has as its primary task the analysis of community structure in terms of division of labor (Hawley 1950).

In the last two decades, scholars of organizations, communities, and societies have called attention to the environment in which such systems exist and survive. This environment includes all things outside the formally structured organization—for example, the weather, geography, and physical social conditions, most of which are outside the control of a given organization. Environment is a major force affecting the birth, maintenance, and death of organizations. Consequently members spend great effort, resources and time to control as much of it as possible. Generally they find little they can do but to accommodate it.

In Arizona, for example, a group of scientists and financiers are attempting such controls in the 90s by experimenting with a biosphere.

In Biosphere 2, a crew of eight persons from several nations are living and working in a sealed environmentally controlled self-contained, self-recycling, three-acre sphere that contains all the factors necessary for life. The air they breathe, the water they drink, the food they eat, and their social order will be sustained by seven enclosed ecological systems designed to replicate the conditions of our world (Biosphere 2 1991).

System Formation and Dependency

Aldrich (1979) attempts to explain this phenomenon of environment by his work dedicated to organizational change featuring the emerging of a concern for relationships between organizations and their environments. He presents an open concept of organizational change that does not take the environment as given and does not assume a completely known or controllable internal structure. The model shifts attention to variables not directly controlled by members of the organization. The model assumes organizations are shaped, pushed, and pulled in directions unintended and unforeseen by members. According to Aldrich, new or changed organizational form occurs as a result of an organizational accommodation of environmental constraints. These constraints may be described as either the resources or information made available to the organization based on member perceptions, such as:

*   Environmental capacity
*   Homogeneity/heterogeneity
*   Stability/instability
*   Concentration/dispersion

* Consensus/descensus

* Degree of turbulence

These environmental constraints affect environmental resource distribution and account for social change and its relevance to organizational change. They also account for how global material and regional affairs affect a local organization's behavior.

The degree of similarity or differentiation between organizations, individuals, and any other social forces directly affect the allocation of organizational resources and the resulting output. A homogeneous environment rewards standardization and leads to undifferentiated products or services. Heterogeneity does the opposite and may lead to interorganizational conflict when standardized products are the goal. The same is true for the environment stability, which leads to stability and continuance of an organization. Stable environment leads to fixed organizational routines and conversely an unstable environment lead to variable organizational behavior.

The degree of environmental interconnectedness (potential or actual) directly affects the capacity of a population to increase the number of organizations it creates to serve its purposes. This is called environmental turbulence. It reflects increased diversity in the interorganizational division of labor.

Loose coupling exists when environment, structure, and activities of parts of an organization or community are weakly connected and therefore free to vary independently. This means one part of an organization or community may change or adapt while others do not.

Such organizational environmental fluctuation and/or accommodations to the environment account for both planned and unplanned adoption of innovations.

Organizations generally attempt to avoid becoming dependent on others, but seek to make other organizations dependent on them. Other organizations are, however, key elements in most organizations' environments. The fact is, organizations must seek out other organizations that control the specialized resources they require for their own organization's existence. This places every organization in a dependent position subject to control of others, despite their efforts to the contrary. The extent of this dependence is related to such factors as formalization, intensity, reciprocity, and standardization of relationships to other organizations outside of their control.

Interorganizational relations is not simply an exchange concept; it involves maintaining a reasonable state of autonomy and avoiding unnecessary dependence. Organizations that are able or willing to vary adaptive strategies for entering into an interdependent environment in fact take advantage of this ever-changing environment to improve their own standing in the population.

As Corwin (1987) notes, all organizations exist in an environment densely populated by other organizations. Mutually dependent organizations form networks among themselves, i.e., a specific social structure consisting of all the connected relationships established by members.

These interorganizational networks or sets are derived constructs of a hierarchical, loosely coupled systems, which can be perceived.

Such interorganizational networks can be identified by tracking down all ties binding organizations in a population.

The concept of loosely coupled systems is essential to comprehending the structure of these interorganizational networks. Network members need not be aware of one another but they are nevertheless interdependent. Members are in continuous negotiation with each other and there is an aggregate pattern of networks. Such patterns include status, hierarchies, interdependence, variations, goal differentiation, and specializations.

This observation is well illustrated by Bidwell and Kasarda (1987) who view an organization as a human ecological community together with its external environment that form an ecosystem, a system in which changing organizational structure and changing environment are reciprocally related. They have developed 100 propositions specifying causal relationships among theories and constructs using Michigan school districts as the network of the study. Bidwell and Kasarda found reciprocal relationships between events in the organizational school environment and its evolving division of labor and hierarchy. This ecosystem theory focuses on relational properties of organizations which they define as ecological communities. Under this model, environment is seen as an array of opportunity for, and constraints upon, change of these relational properties. This too is an open-systems theory where populations in the same community have a common territory defined as environment.

Negandhi (1975) gives a good literature review of closed and open systems, then combines them into three layers or perspectives.

* The organizational environmental layer existing within the closed system which marks location, boundaries, ownership, size, etc.

* The task environment which is conceived of as clients, employees, other groups, public employees, consumers, stockholders, suppliers, distributors, government, and community.

* The societal environmental layer, or the macro environment which includes socio-economic, political, legal, and cultural factors.

He used this theory to study 126 industrial firms in several countries to ascertain the impact of contextual, socio-cultural, and environmental variables on organizations.

Popenoe (1968) argues that social system theory built around such specific properties and hierarchial levels of organized groups must be modified to be applicable to social cultural units such as communities. He believes that the group does not relate to its environment in a subsystem relationship similar to that of organizations because—

* The environment contains much that is unorganized.

* That cultural realities are not all subsumable under nation-state concepts.

* Cultural systems do not fit well into the properties of a social group analysis.

Environmental Dependency

Morgan (1957) noted in his history of the Tennessee Valley Authority that almost no community is wholly isolated from the outside world. In some the contacts are few and infrequent; in other cases the life of the community is so interwoven with that of other communities, societies and organizations that its very individual existence is brought into question.

The point of a unit's dependency on environment was never so evident than in Iraq's experience with the rest of the world in 1991. Over 20 nations, some in traditionally deep conflict with each other, formed a coalition of forces to collectively carry out the Desert Shield/ Desert Storm, operation forcing Iraq to withdraw from the sovereign territory of Kuwait. They did this to challenge Iraq's claim to Kuwait as a province and deep water port.

Sixty Minutes broadcast a television report February 10, 1991, on *Jane's World Military Weapons and Ammunition Handbook (1990)* which included photos, silhouettes, and detail specifications of all military air, ground, and sea vehicles, the weapons they carry, their range-impact, manufacturer, and location throughout the world. Governments of most nations and all superpower nations subscribe to and rely on Jane's information. They cooperate with the publication to provide verification of top secret specifications of each nation's armament. This cooperation among nations has been true through the recent cold war between east and west and will be true through the foreseeable future of our global but still-nationalistic new world. Certainly such a phenomenon gives testimony to the significance of the world's organizational environment and the resulting interdependency of people, their organizations, communities, and nations worldwide.

Rule and Belief Systems

Meyer and Scott (1983), in their elaboration of institutionalized environments including all rules and belief systems, note that rational theories and the relational networks that arise are widely shared. These rules and belief systems provide the normative climate in which formal organizations are expected to flourish in the larger society. Most rules and belief systems are not invented by the organization but brought within its boundaries as a result of diffusion of ideas from their interaction, and activities in everyday situations. Such rule systems are not just "out there" but "in here." Members, participants, clients, and constituents all participate in and are carriers of the culture, thus making institutional environments notoriously invasive. As Pogo might say, "We have met the environment and it is us."

As I have noted earlier, scholarly studies from 1940-1960 emphasized the independence of organizations, while from 1960 to the mid-1970s studies stressed the cultural interdependencies of organizations and their environments. Meyer and Scott conclude that "organizations are affected by the structure of relations of the interorganizational system in which they are embedded, and these systems are in turn affected by the societal systems in which they are located and they are in turn affected by the world system in which they are located" (1983).

Gronbjerg (1989) found, as did Meyer and Scott (1983), that institutionalized belief systems and organizational dependency also shape the behavior of the nonprofit sector. These findings point to the utility of using an ecological perspective when studying a community. Her study suggests we should take a closer look at the very complex inter-actions that exist among public benefit institutions, the communities in which they operate, and the extra-community resources on which they depend. Gronbjerg finds strong indications that such an analysis will significantly extend our understanding of this most complex and inter-esting phenomenon.

Individuals and Their Organizational Environment

Hall (1987) and others have found that organizations are the means by which people are distributed in the social order. He found that the relationship between individuals their organizations and societies, i.e. organization structure and processes, and the environment in which they act, are far more important and useful leads than are leadership, change, or decision-making models in accounting for change and organizational outcomes. He cites empirical research which emphasizes the importance of the environment and presents an overview of structure and processes within organizations that are used to accommodate environments. In addition, Hall found that the more dependent an organization is on its environment the more vulnerable it is; loosely coupled organizations are more adaptive; and all organizations have relationships with other organizations. Interorganizational relations occur for—

*   Procurement and allocation of resources.

*   Formation of political coalitions for advocacy.

*   Achievement of legitimacy or public approval.

Lozano (1990) is one of those writers who love cities, and believes that people's choices of regional identity and a sense of community must be pluralistic and must deal with the cities' total systems environment. He argues that those who would develop cities must promote and develop community-wide objectives aimed at creating a more human environment in which to live and—

*   Regain lost design traditions.

*   Acquire insight on the nature of urban systems.

*   Reverse the current anti-urban cultural trend.

For Lozano, such a community life endeavor should span a continuum of experiences from the climatic urban environment to the more intricate commercial small-scale settlement of neighborhood.

Mega-Crisis and Environment

Mitroff and Tauchant (1990), in an examination of mega-crises to the environment of the world such as Bhopal, Chernobyl, and Exxon Valdez, call for a change in perspective at every level and aspect of society. They argue that these mega-crisis situations represent the intrusion of technology into our very mode of thinking:

*   Our ability to acknowledge intellectually the significance of changes which require people to manage the environment as best they can.

* Our denial at the emotional level of the very need for change. This is particularly true now when eastern block countries are taking the unthinkable actions of experimentation with western style political and economic systems. And now when images and the products of mass media so dominate our society. This is a time when the "craziness" of our human problems seem to be basically the same at the individual, organizational, or societal levels.

In this kind of world, Mitroff and Tauchant now call for a crisis management system to deal with all human-caused mega-crises. Such major crises do not occur because of rational and intellectual limits of people or institutions, as important as they are, but occur primarily because of the emotional and ethical limitations of people and their organizations. Mitroff and Tauchant call this "bounded rationality" which occurs because people and institutions are generally bounded or constrained emotionally and ethically. People are generally limited in their ability to acknowledge situations fraught with extreme conflict, anxiety, and uncertainty. The common misperception that in crises, organizations are not inherently creative, and that they stifle and block member creativity, is only partially true. Mitroff and Tauchant find that organizations can be vastly creative in crisis situations. But when facing trouble, an organization tends to channel this human creativity into activities that sometimes run counter to the main purposes of organization itself as well as society as a whole.

Mitroff and Tauchant argue that mega-crises are not the results of a few bad corporations or faulty management, but that the basic conceptions and principals that govern all organizations operations are inherently flawed and outmoded. Certainly there is much substance to their argument, but I believe Huey (1991) was closer to the mark in his tongue-in-cheek criticism of American universities in his essay *Tenure For Socrates.* In talking about tenure for Socrates, Huey argues that a university that cannot afford truth cannot afford tenure likewise an organization or a society that doesn't recognize or respect truth is in deep trouble.

Huey (1991) points out that all societies are imperfect and in need of critical truth in order to improve, but asks if societies want to improve. American society is the first, if not the only, to declare itself to be a perfect union, but truth that accords well with popular taste and political climate is by definition false. No system improves itself voluntarily against its own immediate interest.

Climate and Culture

Reichers and Schneider (1990) trace the evolution of research on organizational climate and culture from 1929 to the present. They note that both climate and culture deal with ways organization members make sense of their environment in the form of shared meanings that are the basis for their organizational action. Both climate and culture are learned largely through the socialization process and symbolic interaction among members. Organizational climate is viewed only as a lower abstraction of the concepts of culture and subculture. As such, the notions of organizational climate or culture are nothing more than concepts independently developed by researchers over the years that refer to the same things.

Generally, climate is held to be shared perceptions of the way things are around here, or shared perceptions of formal organizational policies, practice, and procedure. Culture is defined as something an organization is or something an organization has.

Reichers and Schneider (1990) reported on recent research efforts that are perceived as being on the cutting edge and advance thinking about conceptual, methodological, and application issues found in the organizational climate and culture literature. They found that whatever goes on in organizations is somehow interpreted by members in a way that has implications for member thoughts, behavior, and organizational performance. All of this translates to what is commonly known as organizational climate or culture.

Chapter 5

ORGANIZATIONS AND INTERORGANIZATION RELATIONS

Organizations are the means by which people are distributed in the social order ... education ... work ... retirement organizational power in society is increasingly interorganizational (Hall 1987).

A community takes concrete form through the organizations that carry out its major functions. As the community evolves, organizations increase in number, scale, and formality. It follows, then, that the main constituents of modern communities are organizations, enough varied organizations so that every individual has the opportunity to become a member of one or more organizations. Through organizational membership each person has the opportunity of becoming a member of a number of communities or societies (Corwin 1987). The distinction that places emphasis on the organization, as opposed to the individual, becomes extremely important in understanding community and the resulting interorganizational phenomenon.

The Individual and the Organization

Gusfield (1975) has noted that distinguishing between groups and individuals as the basis of stratification tends to emphasize the individual with little attention being given to how groups or social units relate to each other, when in fact the individual belongs to a diversity of groups and organizations performing a variety of differentiated roles. Gusfield calls this "segmented pluralities" in which community life is precipitated out into different levels of society.

Galaskiewicz (1979) found, as did (Levine 1972; Turk 1977; Warren et al. 1974; Perrucci and Pilisuk 1970; Loumann and Pappi 1976), that by aggregating individuals into corporate groups or organizations, one can more easily study, explain, and predict behavior of people in their everyday life than if one deals with them just as individuals. Turk (1973) notes that by describing the relationship between the group, its nodes, and linkages in interorganizational work, which are phenomena of the macrosocial order, one can easily shift from macro to micro and vice versa. He found that while the characteristics of individual actors influence the configuration of relationships in the larger social organization, the position of actors in the larger social structures, in turn, directly affects these actors' behavior.

The social philosopher George Mead (1934; Aboulafia 1991) early on in his treatment of self, deals with the phenomenon of cognition consciousness. For him it is the organized community or social group that gives unity to the individual or self. Mead called this phenomenon "the generalized other." The attitude of the generalized other may be defined as the attitude of the whole community.

For Belshaw (1970), differentiation of roles applies to organizations as well as to persons. The division of labor embodied in specialized organizations led to the deep level of complexity of today's communities. Given this profile of modern communities, it is the organized activities of highly specialized organizations that carry out the substance of community activities. These operating networks of organizations constitute the system that carries out the function, the operations, and the policy of community, and ultimately of society as a whole.

Andrews (1984), an engineer and communications expert, helps us make sense of this most complicated phenomenon. He notes that the seemingly rigid institutional hierarchy of society includes a much looser network or smaller interlocking institutional hierarchy that provides rules that allow for competition between organizational networks. These rules tend to winnow out the least appropriate or nonfunctional linkages and enable higher heterogenetic organizational networks to get things done. In effect, the center, the community, or society as a whole does not have to possess—and, in fact, doesn't possess—the overall formal knowledge about how the community or society is organized. No one really knows what or where the center is, or even if there is a center to society, or a community. Communities and societies simply set up an image or criteria of expected performance that members, small groups, and organizations try to fulfill, using whatever strategy or action they think will succeed. The dispersal of control from some mythical center to the multi-organizational sharp end points of the system means, for one thing, that participating members are less likely to revert to social rule-breaking and disobedience. Social rules emerge that reflect reasonably realistic specifications or outcomes required of each organization in the network. Andrew's goal is to establish an interactive communication system between individuals, organizations, communities, and nations, the occurrence of which will yield a high quality of network output that satisfies most, if not all, parties in the system.

Private-Public Relationships

One of the most profound changes in history is the emergence of the concept of a free and independent people becoming organization persons (Emmerich 1978). People look for career, income, and security as employees of stratified organizations in government, business, labor, universities, and voluntary associations. They exercise their sovereignty as individuals and as members of a myriad of organizations, voluntary associations, and interest groups that abound in community life in most of the civilized world.

Emmerich (1978) notes that there is no immaculate separation between the public and private sector, as their fields of activity are becoming increasingly blurred. Large corporations are affected by a public interest and every act of government impinges on a private concern. Official governmental and private interests' authority, are circumscribed by our geniuses for specialization of both role and mission in all types of organizations. For example, the term "bureaucracy" is now generally used in the positive sense of social science, that is, a form of organization under which an increasing amount of the world's work is being carried on. Bureaucracy embodies concepts in the fields of formal and informal structures, group dynamics, communications, and the administrative behavior of all organized activity not just government. The concept of bureaucracy no longer means only the pathology of graft, corruption, favoritism, waste, backwardness, and arrogance of large public or private organizations.

Coalition Dependency

In a political analysis of interorganizational relations, Backarach and Lawler (1980) examined intercoalition formation and intercoalition process in both theory and practice. They did this by forming a hypothesis of expected relationships from these two basic points. They found that the formation or mobilization of interest groups into coalitions formed patterns of conflict as well as cooperation between different coalitions. Consequently, they centered their work on the dimensions of power, authority, influence and how these dimensions affect the politics and bargaining relationships that take place between and among interest groups or organizations in a mobilized coalition. Backarach and Lawler concluded that the power relationship is the most basic and primary mechanism that sub groups and individuals acquire, maintain, and use in coalition formation and operation. There is a continual process of bargaining between and among coalition members relative to each one's action at any time which is based on the power relationships held by each organization member on a given issue at a given time.

The authors concluded that the formal as well as the informal structure of an organization is either a dependent or independent factor in the distribution of power in and across coalitions.   This notion of intercoalition power relationships is grounded to the social exchange concept of dependence where a social network is defined as a patterned set of relationships among actors, groups and organizations in a social space.

The Spiral-Lineal Concept of Social Organization

Matejko (1986) and Young (1988) believe that it is the active participation by individuals in organizations that gives them the chance to grow as persons. In so doing, the individuals become conscious of the far-reaching moral consequences of organizational involvement. Matejko views social conflict among individuals and their organizations as a warning or precursor to change that is natural and unavoidable, and certainly not necessarily negative in consequences. He sees today's organizational microcosm reflective of what he calls the "D-paradigm" of participatory management and organizational life.   For him, such a paradigm is not lineal and static but spiral and dynamic in nature. It implies a lifestyle that links individual life and the culture of society and enables the individual to bargain with the external world and obtain a just share of satisfactions, opportunities, hopes, and self-fulfillment. Each individual actor does so as a member in the active social cultural environment of the organizations of that society.   This is a socio-existential approach to lifestyles.   Matejko argues that the success of a given formal structure depends on the interdependencies already existing in the society, such as—

*   Dependencies and level of socialization

*   Availability of resources

*   Costs of implementation

*   Tradition of participating disciplines

*   Understanding and cooperation of people involved

Under this concept, sociotechnical change is based on the calculation of risks and the actual benefit to each organization. Who will gain, who will lose or change, which values will be given priority—all such relationships change with time and situations. Social realities such as these are fluid and what is done makes people and things quite different, spiral or circular and repetitive in nature rather than lineal or straight-lined and nonrepetitive in nature. Matejko calls this "spiral reasoning" which allows us to see things in their dialectal interrelationship. This is not unlike Young's (1988) metronic society concept with lineal representing the discontinuities of life while the continuities of life are cyclical in nature.

Collaboration in Our Turbulent Environment

The world has become so interdependent and the rate of change so rapid that no organization, large or small, is powerful enough to go it alone. All are operating in a turbulent environment that cannot be dealt with independently. This is true because the turbulence is caused, in large part, by the environment which is outside the direct control of independent organizational managers (Gray 1989).

Gray (1989) suggests collaboration as the best strategy for dealing with problems of a world of growing interdependence. Collaboration is a process in which parties with a stake in the problem actively seek a mutually determined solution within the broader, yet mostly uncontrolled environment in which they operate. Coalitions of independent organizations join forces, pool information, knock heads, construct alternative solutions, and forge agreements aimed at problem solving. Gray's organizational theory attempts to explain why collaboration alliances between business, government, labor, and communities are necessary and warranted. She shows how members of collaborating networks are able to incorporate multiple perspectives to solve their perceived problems. Cooperation, conflict, and coordination, which are a part of the interorganizational collaboration, are viewed as processes where stakeholders assume decision making responsible for their collective futures. The result is that successful, probably innovative, solutions emerge that no single party could have envisioned or enacted. When one party establishes unchallenged power to influence such a phenomenon, collaboration as a process make no sense and will not work and ceases to exist. Collaborations, by definition, involves multiparty distributional issues including fund allocation, standard setting, facility use, and allocations of gains or losses. To coalition members, this collaborative process involves taking risks, which are essential and may yield unfamiliar and unexpected outcomes. Negotiation and mediation activities are essential parts of the process.

Cooperation is the key to almost all forms of interorganizational collaboration. Hall (1987) identifies two types of cooperation. The first is from the outside-in where cooperation is based on the need of coalition members to get a better handle on interdependence relationship in their environment. The second type occurs from the inside-out where cooperation is based on a need to acquire resources for the organization and to establish new interdependencies within the coalition. Such cooperative relationships generally occur as —

* **Ad hoc relationships** that have little or no previous patterning. These cooperative relationships emerge as problems arise and when two or more organizations pool efforts and get together to solve these problems.

* **Exchange relationships** that include any voluntary activity between two or more organizations that lead to cooperation, actual or anticipated, between these organizations in achieving interorganizational goals or objectives.

* **Formalized relationships**, that is, the degree to which cooperation and interdependency among organizations is given official sanction, generally contractual, by the organizations involved.

* **Mandated relationships** that are imposed and governed by some government, law, or regulation.

Coalition interdependence also involves factors such as intensity, frequency, and reciprocity of the power relationships that occur between and among members as they engage in cooperation, conflict, conflict resolution, and the coordination of such relationships.

Kahh and Zald (1990) have noted that this collaborative type of cooperative interdependency also holds at the international level. In the past, international relationships among nations have been assumed by some to lean toward anarchy with the potential power of pitting nation against nation. Such explosive situations are relieved only when dominant nations enforce peace or when potential enemies are so equal in power none dares to interact in open conflict. The recent collapse of the governments in eastern Europe and the Soviet Union and their decision to embrace the western world and its concepts requires an unheard-of international cooperative sophistication; the nations of the world must now learn to manage new forms of interdependence and create organizational structures that can sustain international accommo-dation and cooperation under rapidly changing and dynamic conditions.

This management of interdependence from the interpersonal to national to the interorganizational to the international is what organiza-tions and organization theory is supposed to be all about. It is what adds interest and zest to the field. The invention of organizational forms that enable cooperative relationship among diverse groups has, in fact, been accomplished. This is true in the corporate, academic, religious, and governmental structures of most communities. Change over time has dominated organizations from all sectors of community life and organiza-tions have demonstrated they can and do function without being torn apart by conflicts between departments, divisions, and organizations, despite wide differences in values, subculture, and competition for scarce and limited resources (Kahh and Zald).

Networks and Coalitions

Wilke (1985) has a book of scholarly essays on the theme that coalition formation is the core of social organization. In it intergroup relations are characterized as being like intragroup relations juxtaposed to extragroup coalitions. In this scheme, organizations, not individuals or groups, are viewed as the primary sets of coalitions. Such coalitions are formed because they are generally required to facilitate goal achievement at all levels of society which no one organization is able to achieve alone. The main contribution of this work is the comprehensive view of coalition formation that Wilke presents.

Turk (1977), in a study of the largest cities in the United States, found that activity levels and complexity of newly formed interorganizational networks or coalitions are observable and predictable consequences of existing social integration among organizations that relate in some way to the city. He found that external/local variables predicted the level of such interorganizational activity. He also reports that local integration predicts the complexity found within an interorganizational network. For this study, Turk assumed that organizations are both the formulators and the means that enable individual action; that organizations are the actors in any large and complex structure; and that the communities' roles in large urban settings are defined and enacted by formal groups such as commercial organizations, voluntary associations, governmental and educational agencies, church groups, commissions and public relation departments of large corporations, national and international organizations.

Individual power positions in large cities were found to be determined by and rest heavily upon membership in such organizations. Turk
found the greater the integration of a social setting, the greater is a
community's capacity to support or resist new interorganizational
activities and arrangements. And finally, he found that local integration
as well as external/local integration facilitates organizational activities
and, as such, develop social power within the city.

Aldrich (1979) views concepts such as power, dependency
reciprocity, and intensity among sets and networks of organizations as
governing factors. He notes, however, that with variation among these
dimensions, dependence is usually never at stake or threatened in most
interorganizational transactions; rather, it is enhanced. So, in order to
maintain some sense of autonomy and avoid unnecessary dependence,
leaders and administrators tend to choose strategies for managing
relations within the coalitions they participate in very carefully and very
selectively. Aldrich's concept of organizational networks envisions
environments of the system as multiorganizational aggregates that link
organizations to economic power and social change. For Aldrich, the
major factors that organizations must account for in their environment
are other organizations, because other organizations control the flow of
capital, personnel information and other essential resources necessary for
any organization's existence.

Morgan (1957), as he ponders the value of interdependence for
all individuals, groups, organizations, institutions and nations, notes that
there is more value in the establishment of dependency ties with others

than in independence and autonomy. He argues that organizations, particularly small units, may in fact enhance their normal degrees of sovereignty or independence by their cooperation with other organizations for the common interest of all.

Chapter 6

COMMUNITY COOPERATION AND INVOLVEMENT[1]

*People in groups make a most spectacular "coopera-
tive." Cooperation has over time been steadily
extended in the form of habits of mind. It is the act
of sociability that enables people to ameliorate our
environment and survive* (Young 1988).

This chapter is derived from community-wide efforts at change as
seen by the author in more than 35 years of direct experience in the
business of community development education. It is written to present
core ideas designed to give a clearer understanding of the communities
in which we live. We know, to begin with, that each community has a
history of successful and not-so-successful "community development"
efforts. As a result of these efforts, over time the relationships among
people and between their systems tend to become fragmented and
highly polarized. Positions are taken; sides are drawn as problems arise

---

[1] This work first appeared in *Sociological Practice* Vol. 8, 1990. It is reprinted here with the
Journal's permission.

and are resolved. Conflicting relationships tend to develop among social systems and the people in these systems when their attention is turned to community development problems. The solutions of these problems generally call for significant commitment and cooperation on the part of units (social systems) and people directly affected by the problem.

A Phenomenological Start

As a starting point from which to study the process, we must keep in mind that the community, our community, is what we think it is, what we believe it to be or not to be. If we view our community as good, then that is the way we are going to keep it. If we view it as bad, then we are either going to try to alter it or leave it. How we view our community is related to our belief system. It is phenomenological. It has something to do with perceptions, images, identity, loyalty, and structure (Boulding 1961).

The proposition is made that the community—in terms of its people, social systems, and structure—is a cooperative system, not because cooperation is a "good thing," but because it is absolutely necessary in order to achieve community goals (Kanter 1983; Kelman and Warwick 1973; Loomis 1960; Loumann and Pappi 1976; Parsons 1937, 1960; Weber 1943).

Despite an almost universal impression of national selfishness and narcissism, Americans are basically cooperative. In fact, there is a widely held cultural belief that it is good to be cooperative and bad to be noncooperative. As a society we tend to shy away from or avoid non-cooperative people. But Americans are also pragmatic and discriminate carefully in their patterns of cooperation or involvement. So the basic question is, "Why—that is, in what circumstances and under what conditions—do we cooperate or not cooperate?"

From my scholarship, research, and observation of human behavior, I have worked out this explanation. The general philosophical principle is: I will not cooperate with anybody, for any reason, on any task that I can do myself (Anderson 1963, 1970, 1976, 1986).

I believe that this individualistic, self-centered do-it-myself position characterizes the American people more accurately than participatory democracy, cooperation, altruism, or concern for the well-being of others. When I say this, I am not making a value judgment. I am simply saying analytically that if there is any one principle that seems to govern the behavior of most people, it is the principle that they do not cooperate with anybody on any task they can do themselves.

We all deal with, and are responsible for, very limited resources, the resources of our own time, talent, money, and values. Therefore, it is logical that we ask, "Why should I cooperate?" before making a cooperative commitment.

Clearly, we cannot always remain independent because we haven't the resources to do everything alone. We organize and cooperate to achieve tasks that we perceive are worth doing and that we cannot achieve by ourselves. If any one of us could do these tasks individually we probably would, because then the benefits derived from them would be ours—social recognition, monetary reward, self-satisfaction, or whatever—benefits based on values of importance to us. If I cooperate with somebody on a task, then it is no longer my project, it is our project. I must share the gains or losses associated with it with somebody else.

Once we identify a project worth doing and assess what is needed to get the job done, the relevant principle of involvement is that the only time we should seek the involvement of someone else is when he or she has a resource that, combined with our resource, will accomplish the task that could not be independently achieved. Even then we tend to share or exchange primarily our loosely held or surplus resources, but not our closely held values.

All acts of involvement have a price tag, a cost, an investment, a responsibility. This cost is reflected in terms of the allocation of our own limited resources and our identification with the resulting product. So when we set up cooperative arrangements, these are not to be entered into lightly. None of us can afford to be so cooperative as to say, "Sure, count me in," every time we are asked to become involved in an activity. That may be why there appears to be some public apathy in most communities. It may well be that many of our community projects are really not worth the cost of commitment called for or necessary to complete the project. Maybe the costs, or the potential losses, are too high. Or it simply may be a project of little or no importance to us at that time. In other words, cooperation may be good and rewarding, not so good and not rewarding, or irrelevant and unnecessary. In fact, it may be harmful (Etzioni 1975; Kimberly et al. 1980; March 1965; March and Simon 1959; Merton 1959).

We do not really involve ourselves in any meaningful decision making, development, or cooperative act without committing ourselves and our resources to that action. To simply say, "It is a good idea," or "I wish you luck," or "Let me know how it turns out," is not meaningful interaction; it is not cooperation and does not generally lead to development. Only when we are willing to invest ourselves and our resources are we likely to become a part of community decision making and community development. When we do this, we place our life's values on the line and they generally cannot be retracted. That is what it takes to get into the decision-making structures of communities and to become a community decision maker for community development. Our personal and organizational resources — name, reputation, what we stand for — are involved.

The Cooperative Process

Community involvement is a very obvious part of community development. Community involvement, by definition, calls for community cooperation. But what is "cooperation" (Barnard 1938)? Cooperation is a very widely used and generally misunderstood concept in most communities of America. It is appropriate, at this point, to state my ideas about community cooperation in a more precise form:

* Cooperation is not good or bad; it may be either or both.

* Community action is organizational in character, whether it is the informal organization of two people or large-scale formal organizations of 500 people. Community action is an organizational activity and, as such, some common "principles of organization" govern the action.

* Community actions are interorganizational and therefore cooperative activities. This is true not because of choice or

because of the goodness or appropriateness of cooperation, but because of a necessity for multi-person/multi-unit involvement and commitment for successful community problem resolution.

*   Cooperation is the ordinary business of life in a human society.

*   Cooperation comes into being when (1) there are persons or organizations able to communicate with each other (2) who are willing to contribute their own limited resources to a cooperative action (3) to accomplish a specific goal.

*   Cooperation occurs only when individual or organizational limitations become significant factors in goal achievement and when the application of the resource energy of two or more persons or organizations has the potential to overcome this limitation.

People must be induced to cooperate or there can be no cooperation. The net satisfactions that induce people to contribute their efforts to an organization result from their perception of positive advantages as against the disadvantages that are entailed. Sufficient conditions for involvement in cooperative community action programs involve at least three elements or postulates:

Postulate 1:
An individual or organization will become involved in, and contribute resources to, cooperative activities that will directly enhance the interest of that specific individual or organization.

Postulate 2:
An individual or organization will become involved in, and contribute resources to, cooperative activities that will directly

enhance the interest of a broader community of interests of which that specific individual or organization is a member or part.

When these two conditions are met, it is possible to postulate that:

Postulate 3:
An individual or organization will insist on becoming involved in and contributing resources to cooperative activities that are perceived as serving the actual or potential good of the whole community of interest as well as of each individual or organization holding membership in that community.

The Involvement Process

Given this image of the cooperative process, I now want to describe briefly a model for community involvement. To do so, I have drawn heavily on the work of a number of sociologists at Michigan State University. I believe their work provides a base for understanding community involvement as it really is (Sower et al. 1957; Miller 1953). There are four major elements to the model:

* Problem recognition, convergence of interest and goal formation

* Identification of a problem

* Identification of the individual units and groups directly affected, positively as well as negatively

* Development of alternative solutions

* Establishment of an initiating set

* Justifying the membership of the initiating set

* Justifying the goals proposed by the initiating set

* Securing legitimation, support, and sponsorship of these goals

* Recruitment and establishment of an execution set

* Justifying the membership of the execution set

* Securing organizational as well as individual commitment to a program of action

* Planning the detailed course of action to follow

* Implementing or carrying out the action program

Briefly let us follow the path through this model for community involvement (Figure 5) and see if it has any relevance to the understanding of community action programs. I believe it does account for and explain essential aspects of most community action projects. Note that all of the "action" in this model takes place before the implementation of the community action.

Let us assume a community problem has been recognized and alternative courses of action have been contemplated. Starting at the top of the model, our first task is to identify the specific social units (the social structures) that in one way or another are directly affected by the community action to be taken. Make a list of all individuals, groups, or organizations that have a socially defined right to become involved in the action. At this point it is not important how or if they will get involved or what position (for or against) they are likely to take. The only test to be met is: do they have the socially defined right to be involved in the action?

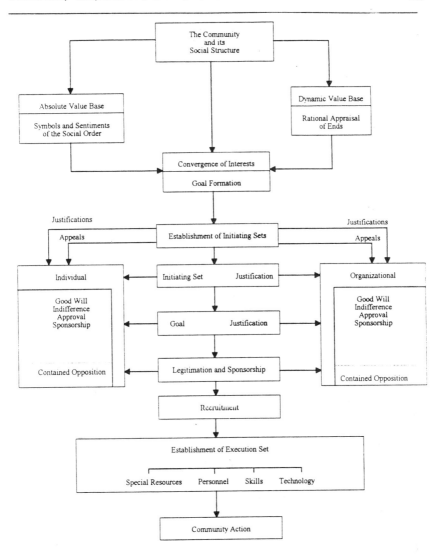

Figure 5. *Model for community involvement*

If so, they make up the **legitimate order** affected by that particular problem. The legitimate order is defined as including all individuals or groups who see themselves and are seen by others as having the socially defined right to be involved in the action. One test of such membership is whether the unit in question will go into opposition and allocate resources to fight the action if it is ignored, not consulted, or not involved.   .

Next we need to consider the basis for securing cooperation of members of the legitimate order for the community action proposed. Support for such action must logically evolve from value bases appropriate to each unit in the legitimate order of the social structure within which it is being proposed. In fact, that each organization in the legitimate order will independently test--approve or reject--the proposed action using its own organizational values as involvement criteria.

The value bases for cooperative involvement of these units are derived from two sources. The first I call the **absolute value base**, such as "symbols and sentiments"; the second may be referred to as the **dynamic value base**, such as "appraisal and allocative standards."

Symbols and sentiments are considered to be absolute in character. They are the time-tested, traditional, generally unchallengeable foundations of an individual's or an organization's behavior. They are belief systems. Every individual and organization has a belief system, an absolute value base that is not challengeable. To debate it is nonsense. If, for example, I am bigoted and a racist, you are not going to change my mind or my heart with logical reasoning and arguments that assert that I shouldn't be. You may be able to do it with some other kinds of strategy, but probably not with rational debate or systematic evidence. This value base may govern whether and how I do or do not become involved in cooperative activity.

Dynamic values, or appraisal and allocative standards, on the other hand, are rationally derived, tentative in nature, and subject to periodic evaluation and change. They are best illustrated by our use of new knowledge. As technology develops, we drop old technologies and old ways of doing things and adopt new ways, employing the new technology. Such value changes are ever-present and occur in all facets of life. We see evidence of this in the market place, in the food we eat and the fashions we wear. We see it in modes of travel, offices, and industry. We even see changes in education, religion, and community affairs.

After the assessment of value bases likely to govern the behavior of the social structure to be involved, the next step in the model is the convergence of interest. This takes on a special meaning here in that it implies a convergence upon the acceptance of a specific group goal. Different individual organizations can accept the same goal for quite different reasons. The important point is that convergence does take place regardless of the individual or independent motive backing this social convergence. When social convergence takes place, then, and only then, does meaningful goal formation occur.

In many community development efforts, however, the tendency is to deal with the people who have the same values we have, those who have to contribute essentially the same resources that we possess. We hesitate to talk to those who have a different set of values; we find it uncomfortable and difficult to associate with them. We have difficulty understanding their positions. In essence, we tend to talk to ourselves, never really recognizing that there are .other views in the world. If we really want to solve community problems, we must involve people with different viewpoints—and on their terms, not ours.

In so doing, we will modify our goal a little bit to accommodate their vested interests. To the extent that points of common interest can be enhanced or solved by a community action proposal, we can expect to secure a positive commitment of cooperation from the relevant units. If, on the other hand, we push for action and such a move is perceived as detrimental or upsetting to these vested interests, organized opposition to the plan will probably take shape. It also is entirely possible to propose a project that affects relevant units but, in their view of the situation, the potential impact seems inconsequential, so they are indifferent to the project and take no action.

The decision to cooperate or not cooperate made by each unit involved is determined by some combination of absolute values and dynamic values. There is not much room to argue or debate the first. It is generally not advisable to tamper with symbols and sentiments or belief systems. If our proposal fits, it will generate support. If not, we cannot do much to change the situation. Isolation of such units in the legitimate order may be called for. The use of reason or debate, when the proposal is counter to the organization's symbols and sentiments, could well result in the generation of dedicated opposition rather than cooperation. On the other hand, appraisal and allocative standards or dynamic values can be changed with the proper presentation of sound rational and factual information.

When we attempt to induce an organization to cooperate in community action programs, the main points to remember are:

* Select symbols and sentiments common to each organization for use in the appeal for cooperation.

* Select symbols and sentiments independently held that are not in conflict with other organizations' interests.

* Do not directly alter or attempt to change organizational symbols and sentiments that run counter to the proposed plan of action. Try to avoid them; it is generally better to "go it alone" than stir up dedicated opposition.

* Select common appraisal and allocation standards when possible.

* Aggressively counter conflicting appraisal and allocation standards with hard factual evidence and you will establish a new base for cooperative efforts.

I want to underscore again the point that the decision to become involved, to cooperate, is made by each unit of the legitimate order on **its own value terms**, not ours.

After we have accounted for vested interests, we can move to the next step: the establishment of an **initiating set**. This is a group of individuals or organizations who are held in high enough regard to have the social right to initiate a plan of action. They also must be able to legitimize the plan and secure the obligation of others in the sponsorship of action. The right of an individual or an organization to initiate, to introduce something in a community, has to be earned; it is not granted automatically. Here is where many community development efforts run into program difficulties. What kinds of activities does that group have the right to initiate with the community? What activities are strictly not their right to become involved in? For example, presidents of universities have the right to raise money for teaching and research, but they are not the right people to initiate changes in the curriculum. That is a faculty responsibility. Preplanning the correct strategy to use is essential at this stage of the process.

The initiating set also has to justify its goal in terms of value bases. As mentioned above, findings on community action show clearly that different individuals and organizations justify group goals for quite different or even opposing reasons. The important test is not how each group justifies the goal, but whether or not it does, and whether it then decides to join in the sponsorship of the action.

An important function of the initiating set in the involvement process is to conduct negotiations to determine how to alter and redefine the goal so as to involve the critical proportion of the legitimate order that can justify, legitimize, and, hence, sponsor and support the proposed action.

Moving to the lefthand block of the model, we see that individuals will either offer good will, support, be indifferent to, or oppose the proposed action. Likewise, we see on the righthand block of the model that organizations have the same alternatives. How access to different individuals or organizations in the legitimate order is to be gained— whether by overlapping or multimembership in different organizations, personal channels, justification based on logical reasoning, or by some other kind of general appeal—must be determined and carried out by the initiating set at this stage of the involvement process.

To begin with, the initiators need to account for major organized interests that potentially have something at stake in such a goal effort. These may be classified into at least three groups: approving, indifferent, and opposed. The point here is to actually identify and specifically account for the kind of involvement that can be expected from the individual and organized interests directly affected by the action proposal.

Early strategy to follow would be the neutralization or containment of potential opposition and the moving of indifferent individuals and organizations into a position of supportive involvement in goal formation and program sponsorship. This can be accomplished by carefully justifying the proposed plan using the independent value bases governing the behavior of each individual or organization. It may be that one of the best sources of assistance in goal formation, sponsorship, and execution leadership can be obtained from what are initially indifferent individuals and organizations. If the opposition is not contained or neutralized at this point in the process, common sense would say the plan should be brought to a halt and a reappraisal made.

Community action programs traditionally are perceived as being carried out by community leaders, community-minded individuals. I would argue, however, that most action programs call for commitments of resources far beyond those held by individuals. If we are trying to achieve anything that has an impact, not only do we have personal commitments of individuals, but we also have to secure corporate or organizational commitment, large and small, public and private, and vertical as well as horizontal. Many projects call for commitment of the scarce resources of the city, churches, utilities, associations, industrial and business firms, schools, colleges, and universities. Unless we obtain such commitment, we are not likely to activate a meaningful program. Rather, we will probably engage in a lot of talk, have a lot of dialogue, but have no action program.

It is individuals who in the end must represent their organization and commit its resources for or against the proposed action. It should not be too difficult to identify the individuals who, as responsible organizational representatives, can justify and sponsor an action program within their own organization. They must not only be personally committed, but must be able to justify the program to their representative organization and secure an organizational commitment of support.

After the decision is made to carry out or execute the action, it is important to obtain the necessary facilities for carrying it out. This is accomplished through what can be called the recruitment process. This is the point at which firm commitments for cooperative action are made, and execution set is formed and carries out the details of the action plan.

Winding It Up

As we attempt to mobilize resources for our program, I would like to suggest that we secure only the resources sufficient to get the job done. I question the advisability of always attempting to maximize involvement. I do so on several grounds:

* We are always dealing with limited resources of people's time, talent, and economic possessions. We must be discriminating in our allocation of these resources.

* There are many good alternative community development projects that call for citizen and corporate or organizational involvement. To expect extensive, continuous commitment of people for all "good causes" is to expect the impossible.

* For some projects, widespread involvement may, in fact, prevent rather than facilitate community goal achievement. When the task becomes everybody's responsibility, in all too many cases it becomes nobody's responsibility.

* There is a social cost associated with involvement. You can go to the social bank of good will and withdraw people's commitment and involvement only for a limited period without making some new deposits.

Finally, I wish to restate the basic questions that must be answered if you are to secure cooperative involvement of people and their organizations in community development programs:

* What specific tasks are you attempting to achieve?

* What kind of involvement is really necessary to get the job done?

* What contribution will each involved person or organization be expected to make, when, and can they afford to make such a contribution?

* What is in it for them?

* What is in it for you?

* What is in it for your community?

Chapter 7

THE DEMOCRATIC MODEL OF PARTICIPATION EXAMINED[1]

There is a worldwide search by individuals in every walk of life and on every continent for more direct and adequate ways of expressing themselves and of influencing the course of events (Siegel 1969).

Current "participation" concepts, so dramatically and aggressively fought for in the ghettos, streets, colleges, churches, and individual organizations, derive from our belief in the tenets of "participatory democracy" in the decision-making process. Decision making is an ongoing social process defined as the reduction of alternative courses of action by an actor or actors in the decision-making system (Miller 1952). For most, participation is held to be an inalienable and individual right along with our freedom of speech, press, and religion. Not only is it a right, but it is "good." For most, then, the question of participation is not

---

[1]This work first appeared in the *Journal of the Community Development Society*, Vol. 1, no. 2, Fall 1970. It is printed here with the Journal's permission.

whether there should be participation, but rather, how, when, and to what extent participation should function to produce the best decisions. This is the essence of our "democratic model of participation."

But as Spiegel and Mittenthal (1968) put it:

> *Truly, the more one explores the endless ramifications of citizen participation, the more one appreciates the old adage of 'moving a tiger by the tail.' Every effort to reduce its [amoeba-like] substance to a definable, systematic, and comprehensible body of thought is resisted by inherent dilemmas, contradictions between myth and reality, and even between different sets of observable social phenomena. . . . If one concludes . . . that citizen participation is, by nature, good and desirable, then nearly every instance of it demonstrates a modicum of value. . . [yet] if one has reservations about the efficacy of the process, it is not difficult to substantiate such doubts* (Spiegel et al., 3-4).

Despite the overwhelming evidence of bias clouding our analysis of the concept of participation, I cannot resist tipping my hand prematurely and asserting that, for me, participation, like cooperation, is neither good nor bad; it may be either or both. More importantly, participation and its administration in social systems is simply absolutely necessary in order to arrive at workable and implementable decisions in complex organizations, associations, and communities that characterize today's world.

De Tocqueville (1945) asserted that association-type, voluntary participation in America characterizes our way of life; it has become habit. It is the way decisions are made and actions carried out; likewise, association-type, voluntary participation in decision making is part of our democratic model or participation. But is it in real life? Or should it be?

For example, how widespread is citizen participation in decision making? Is citizen participation general, or is it limited to specified segments of our population?

Research findings (Wright and Hymn 1958; Rosenthal 1967) show that the higher the socioeconomic status of the population, the greater their level of citizen participation in associations and in community decision making. Bloomberg and Rosenstock (1968), in their analysis of the "maximum feasible participation" concept, call attention to the fact that, contrary to the popular stereotype, the majority of American citizens of any class generally belong to few organizations; most tend to be passive members rather than the active core of those organizations; and, moreover, only a small proportion of those associations affect or normally become involved in community decision making.

Citizens in mass are rarely involved in community decisions other than those made through referendums and elections. As Dahl (1967) notes, "Most citizens use their political resources scarcely at all." Furthermore, most research, such as that of Sills (1957), shows that individual memberships in associations, as well as decision-making bodies in general, are invited, "sought out," rather than voluntary or self-appointed.

There can be no argument, however, over the fact that today's society is an organizational society, that persons who set out to achieve goals form associations very early in the process with other people in order to complete the task. They form organizations to mobilize resources and to maintain control of the process. As I have pointed out organizations are the basic social unit responsible for development.

Organizations are control mechanisms through which power for development is generated and flows.

I believe that one of the most human aspects of our life is our profound desire and ability to control our environment, everything that exists about us. What we see, what we can reach, we manipulate and deal with as we come in contact with it. Our drive for power and control through organization is manifest in many forms, including developments in education, business, industry, as well as in civil rights activities of the type espoused by Martin Luther King, the pragmatic, mass-power-based People's Organization of Saul Alinsky, or the militant activities of the Weatherman faction of Students for a Democratic Society.

The development of power and the control or administration of it through association or organization is the reason for participation. Participation through organization generates power for the individual as well as the organization.

Galbraith (1967) notes that within the past 50 years, power and its administration have shifted from land and capital holders to ". . . association(s) of men of diverse technical knowledge, experience, or other talent. . . ." The exercise of power now extends from the leadership of our modern industrial enterprises down to the unskilled worker at the bottom of the labor force and welfare recipients. It embraces a large number of people possessing a wide variety of talent.

The generation and control of power are critical aspects of participation in decision making. Taylor (1979) points out in his discussion of Model Cities programming that "control is a word that permeates the rhetoric of the minority community and is rarely, if ever, heard in the white community." His assessment is that minorities' concern for control is in large part simply a rhetoric of self-affirmation, reflected in the Black Power movement and the Mexican-Americans' grape boycott. These efforts, like those of the early labor movement, represent attempts to mobilize and control power from a homogeneous resource base.

But as Taylor (1979) points out, there can be no exclusive control by citizens or by any single citizens group. He describes the Model Cities concept of participation as a combination of public and private forces working together in partnership, with the city clearly as the dominant partner. In this program, citizens and city government negotiate a sharing of power and control. Taylor states three principles that undergird the Model Cities concept of participation, which I believe have relevance to the citizens model of participation.

* Power must be shared in reality, not just on paper.

* The purpose of power sharing must be positive—to identify and meet real needs, and to develop the capacity to function effectively in a society where coalitions, not absolutes, control.

* Success will be determined by the way persons work together, not the rhetoric that often tears them apart.

Both the Detroit riots of 1967 and the New Detroit Committee's work to put the city back together after the riot well illustrate the principle that communal issues can, and often must, be solved with the power generated by participation and sharing of control by heterogeneous and even incongruous citizens and groups.

The New Look

The need to organize has to be recognized before participation will, in fact, occur. Issues trigger concern and need for participation. They serve as the common rallying point for inducing participation. More often than not, the issues emerge in a dramatic fashion, precipitated by a specific event or occurrence which is the culmination of a veritable iceberg of under-surface events (Spiegel 1969).

In the Detroit riots of 1967, the trigger was a rather routine police raid on an after-hours "blind pig" establishment. The resulting participation in rebuilding the city socially as well as physically is now history in the making.

Using this very limited review of critical aspects of our democratic model of participation as a base, we now turn to a model of participation as I see it; I call it a *returns model of participation*.

The model was triggered by my discovery that currently accepted "principles" associated with our democratic model of participation administration in organization decision making are little more than ambiguous and mutually contradictory proverbs. For almost every reported principle of participation, an equally plausible and accepted contradictory principle can be found that leads to exactly opposite organizational recommendations. There appears to be nothing in current literature to indicate which is the proper principle to apply to a given situation at a given time.

The returns model is put forward in the hopes it will add order and give understanding to the application of general principles of participation in decision making. It represents an effort to meet, in part, the need for a theoretical rationale that will add objectivity (rationality) to administration of participation in the decision making of social systems.

While the environment of decision making is ever-changing, the model proposed is static. It assumes, for purposes of analysis, that a recognized dynamic social system may be frozen at any given time. It assumes perfect knowledge at that time. The model also assumes that certain variables may be fixed (controlled), allowing for measurement of effects obtained from varying inputs of non-fixed (treatment) variables. In this model, the treatment variable of concern is units of participation. A participation unit is considered to be a written or verbal, factual or judgmental input (by an individual or a team of people), which directly affects the decision made and its implementation.

The model is based on the premise that decision making is the science of choice (Heady 1957). The specific aspect of the decision-making process that it deals with is the allocation of limited participation inputs within an organizational setting. In reality, choices are made on the basis of imperfect knowledge and an uncertain future; they involve challenge and risk. This tool, when properly used, should help reduce the risk involved in decisions by providing a theoretical basis for selecting the individuals or teams of people who should participate in such decisions.

The participation returns model starts with a concept that Galbraith (1967) calls the synthesis by organization of a "group personality" in decision making. Group-type participation in decision-making is necessary in order to gather the specialized, scientific, or technical information that is held by many separate individuals.

The following conditions are basic to this concept of participation:

* Participation of individuals or teams of people must be induced, generally through invitation.

* Participation must be by people with heterogeneous inputs.

* Participants must bring limited, highly specialized knowledge or skill to the decision-making process.

* Individual or team participants must be involved only in limited and specific areas of the total process.

* The timing of their participation in the process is critical.

The goal of the decision-making process is to render a decision that has a high probability of being implemented and producing the desired results. Initially, the administration of this model calls for adding just enough participation units in the decision-making process to render the decision and activate it. To qualify as a participant, an individual or team must make a unique contribution to the process. This contribution must be necessary to the successful rendering of the decision and its activation. The contribution is a necessary one if its removal would cause the decision-making process to fall apart or fail.

The slogan that seems best to describe this sufficiency test of participation would be *minimum feasible participation*, as opposed to the more popular concept of *maximum feasible participation*.

As I see it, in the initial stages of the process we should not be concerned with maximizing participation, efficiency, effectiveness, or anything else. The first priority should be given to "birth" and "survival." If we can order the administration of participation units so that at least one unit of product emerges as a result of the decisions rendered, we will have reached the theoretical level of survival. We will have a system that works, one that does what it was designed to do. After we discover that it works, there is time enough to be concerned about maximizing efficiency, effectiveness, and even participation.

The model is derived from two basic types of returns. The first, *increasing returns*, occurs when the productivity of each additional unit of input or variable factor applied to all other required or fixed factors adds more to the total return than the previous input unit. This principle may be illustrated graphically (see Figure 6) as a curve convex to the origin or axis type of function. The total return curve or the input-return relationship is one where total return increases at an increasing rate when successive input units are added.

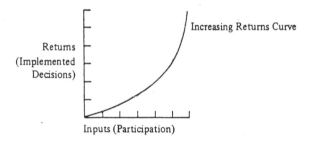

Figure 6. *Increasing returns*

When participation in decision making is the input factor, when all other factors required in the decision-making process are held constant, and when implemented decisions are the returns, we see that the increasing return relationship is commonly found in the decision-making process. For example, in a Model Cities program, which has little or no provision for citizen participation in planning decision making, the addition of more units of citizen participation will probably result in an increasing return to the decision-making process, i.e., a higher probability of rendering an implementable decision. Such participation contributes criticism, corrective insight, and continuing validation to decision-making effort (Cahn and Cahn 1968).

Edelston and Kolodner (1968) provide some empirical evidence that citizen participation of the poor in OEO program planning contributes to better planning and decision making when, and only when, participants are provided the opportunity to comprehend what is happening. This condition requires the additional inputs of time, money, and a method to facilitate a process that is more than perfunctory. They caution that participation without these conditions disintegrates into meaningless ritual.

The second type of returns, *diminishing returns*, occurs when the productivity of each additional input unit or variable factor applied to all other required or fixed factors adds less to total return, i.e., a reduction in the probability of rendering an implementable decision, than the previous input unit. This principle may be illustrated graphically (see Figure 7) as a curve concave to the origin or axis type of function. The total returns curve or input-return relationship is not a straight-line linear function due to the fact that the total return may increase at a decreasing rate, or decrease at an increasing rate, or result in a negative return when additional input units are added.

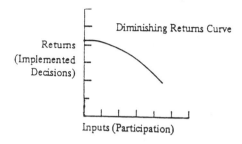

Figure 7. *Diminishing returns*

The diminishing returns relationship is commonly found in the decision-making process, and may also be illustrated using the problem of Model Cities planning. After certain levels of participation inputs of citizens, planners, elected officials, and technical consultants in the decision-making process are reached, the addition of more input units — more citizens, more planners, or more elected officials — actually becomes dysfunctional. Recognition of this consequence is reflected in Taylor's (1969) suggested principles guiding administration of Model Cities programs. It is also consistent with Cahn and Cahn's (1968) empirical findings in an examination of eight different community issues in hundreds of cities. Their conclusions tend to support the contention that unlimited and indiscriminatory citizen participation can immobilize successful decision making. In fact, several essays in the book of reading in which the Cahns' work appeared (Spiegel and Mittenthal 1968), convince me that adding more and more participation units to the decision-making process will, at some point, cause diminishing returns to the process.

The Returns Model

The types of return discussed rarely occur as separates; rather, they are generally combined into a total return relationship called in most economic textbooks the *total product curve or function*. Here I have applied this relationship to the decision-making process, calling it the *returns* model (Figure 8).

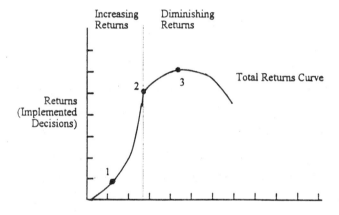

Figure 8. *The returns model*

Figure 8 illustrates increasing and decreasing returns to decision making when the single variable input factor is participation and all other required or fixed factors are held constant (any number of variable factors in relation to any combination of fixed factors of decision making may be dealt with by the model). When ordered in this fashion, all returns functions may be accounted for. This it an approach that systematically utilizes and accounts for the entire range of valid, yet seemingly

seemingly contradictory, principles and factual data related to participation in decision making.

Starting from point 0, as units of variable input (participation units) are added, the first unit of output (implemented decisions) occurs at point 1. As more participation units are added, the total output curve continues to rise at an increasing rate to point 2, the point of maximum efficiency of inputs in relation to output (implemented decision). When still more units of participation are added, the rate of increase of the total output curve slows progressively to point 3, which is the point of return maximization or maximum effectiveness of participation in decision making. Thereafter, the total output curve declines with the addition of more participation unit inputs until zero output is reached.

It is my firm belief that because of our dedication to the "goodness" and "rightness" of participation in decision making, we as scholars and community development specialists tend to overstress and over-invest in participation unit inputs. We keep adding inputs long after point 3 is reached, only to experience negative returns from our efforts (good programs that don't come off). Given my preference for *minimum feasible participation*, I would urge those of us committed to the achievement of essential social development goals like those of Model Cities to strive initially for participation in decision making at the point 1 level and work toward point 2 before we become addicted advocates of *maximum feasible participation* in the decision making of society.

Chapter 8

HOW TO ORGANIZE FOR INVENTIVENESS

Technical progress and organizational development are aspects of one and the same trend in human affairs; and the persons who work to make these processes actual are also their victims (Burns and Stalker 1961).

History records that developments in power, agriculture, medicine, engineering, and chemical technology occurred alongside the development of working organizations. This trend brought with it elaboration of organizational communication networks with complex mechanisms of economic, political, and social control. Innovations and development in technology and/or social organization have often been by way of adaption to changes in one or the other, or both. Development carries the connotation of change which in turn implies risk. The value of change is often equated with or weighed against other risks arising from maintaining the *status quo*. Concern about development is a condition of human existence and is articulated in the institutions and procedures of our sophisticated technological industries, for creation and innovation are an essential component of most industrial and business enterprises.

The interdependence of material technology and social organization is made explicit by a study of 20th century invention and innovation. For today, invention, even more than science, is a social phenomenon, in quite matter-of-fact ways, it is a human activity which can only be fulfilled when certain social conditions obtain (Burns and Stalker 1961).

Whitehead (1933) has said that the greatest invention of the 19th century was the invention of the method of invention. Burns and Stalker (1961) contend that the 20th century has brought with it the discovery of how to organize inventiveness. The difference between the two statements is not so much the nature of inventions or inventors, but rather the manner in which the context of social institutions are organized for their support.

For most of human history, invention was largely autonomous and dependent upon isolated individuals. But in the last few decades, an industry of discovery has developed substantial resources (more than $10 billion per year in the United States alone) and large-scale organizations are now devoted to invention (Dunlop 1962). This phenomenon has been called the art of organized forcing of technological change. In this chapter we shall hold that organization for inventiveness, change, or development is more than an art; it is now a systematic, scientifically reproducible phenomenon. The development organization concept offers an explanation of how we organize for inventiveness. One example of such an organization is the Michigan Livestock Health Council.

For our purpose, an organization may be viewed as a system of cooperative human activities and resources, the function of which are the creation, transformation, and exchange of utilities. It is a group of highly specialized individuals, working together in a structured manner, dedicated to achieve specific defined goals. An organization comes into being only when individual resource limitations become significant factors in goal achievement and when the consolidated resources of two or more persons will overcome the individual's limitations. The expenditure of specialized consolidated resources in a structured goal-oriented activity is what adds purpose and power to organized systems.

A development organization may be viewed as a structured grouping of people or a formal organization dedicated to develop at least one specific goal which cannot be achieved by the individuals or organizations independently. Organizational resources are significant limiting factors that prevent independent organizational goal achievement. In order to achieve such goals, a development organization must be created to gain access to the specialized resources of a multiplicity of other participant-recipient social systems. A *participant-recipient* system is defined as any social system, formal or informal, that either contributes resources for or receives the benefit from such goal achievement efforts of a development organization or both. The organizations of the system do not merge or in any other way give up their individual autonomy.

Development organization personnel, without the aid of position or chain of command authority, must gain access to resources of participant-recipient systems across bureaucratic social system boundaries. The strength of their influence is reflected in the participant-recipient systems' perceptions of an interest, and the willingness and ability of the development organization and its personnel to facilitate achievement of common development goals.

Development organization goals must therefore be perceived as for the good of participant-recipient systems that either contribute to or benefit from such goal achievement as perceived independently by each unit in the participant system. Both the participant-recipient system and the development organization must justify this cooperative action and sharing of resources within their own beliefs, sentiments, values, and patterns of social organization. The relationship is illustrated in Figure 9.

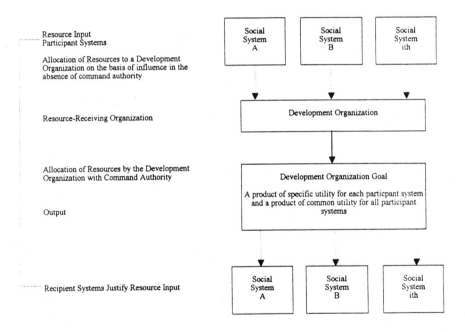

Figure 9.   *A model of development organization activity*

There are at least two ways that any two or more organizations can establish cooperative working relationships: (1) they merge certain portions of themselves in such a manner as to operate as a single integrated unit subsidiary to one of the major cooperating systems, or (2) they agree to act on common goals yet retaining autonomous organizational identities at all times. A development organization, by definition, establishes its cooperative working relationships with participant-recipient systems by use of the second alternative. A development organization never merges with or acts as a subsidiary of other social systems. It simply gains access to resources of these systems and independently allocates these resources to common development efforts.

In effect, when a participant-recipient system invests resources into a development organization, it grants to the management and personnel of the development organization all power to use the resources to create and produce development goals. At this point the participant-recipient system transfers all direct control over the product to the development organization. They simply reserve the right to receive a portion of the rewards or costs resulting from the creation of the development product.

The management within the development organization now holds all the power to use or allocate the resource assets collected from participant-recipient systems. Management is free to use these resources in any way it deems proper to the creation and production of a development product of utility. Management receives this authority from the participant-recipient systems on the basis of influence ascribed to the development organization.

This allocation of authority is not really a matter of choice on the part of either the participant-recipient system or management of the development organization. Forty-five, twenty-five, or even five, viable, autonomous, sometimes competing organized special interest groups would find it difficult, if not impossible, to collectively manage anything. No large enterprise could possibly go forward except under a unified and concentrated system of organization and command.

The concentration of the specialized resources of the many participant-recipient systems under the single command of the development organization management creates the power to produce a development product. When these two conditions are met, the phenomenon of power to transfer resources of one level of utility to resource products of a higher level of utility occurs. This exchange transformation and creation of utilities could not have been achieved by the development organization alone, by independent participant-recipient systems, or by direct merger of one or more of these systems.

In fact, if one or more of the participant-recipient systems should attempt to hold a command authority over the development organization and its product, all other participant systems could and probably would (1) withdraw their resources, thus rendering goal achievement impossible, or (2) discredit the product developed by devaluating its utility.

Organizations that have achieved technological advancements in agriculture, engineering, medicine, etc., all exhibit a high degree of organizational independence. In fact, the main reason they exist is to develop specific products of utility that can be differentiated from all similar products produced by other similar functional systems. The clear distinction between the function and products of an organization provides the means for its survival. Primacy and autonomy of function forms the link between that organization and the larger social system of society. This autonomy is derived from and is functional in light of the special values that brought about the creation of that organization. However, autonomous organizational values of several independent organizations within an interdependent social framework leads to inter-organizational conflict. At first glance, this interorganizational conflict can be viewed as an intolerable condition that tends to reduce the efficiency of organized development efforts. However, in this chapter we postulate that organizational values in conflict are contributory and many times necessary conditions of organized change and inventiveness. Autonomous organizational values in conflict are therefore viewed as contributory and many times a necessary condition for development.

Litwak and Hylton (1962) offer an interorganizational theory that suggests the structural requisites necessary for maintaining what they call "socially approved conflict." They point out that within a community consisting of several autonomous yet interdependent organizations, the breakdown or elimination of interorganizational conflict is likely to disrupt sound interorganizational relations. This socially approved conflict is governed by mechanisms that tend to standardize interorganizational actions of autonomous units of organization. By contrast, many analyses of intraorganizational relationships assume that conflicting values lead to a breakdown in organizational structure. The separation of interorganiza-tional and intraorganizational analysis sensitizes the correlates of value conflict and value consistency between and within organizations. This separation allows for an understanding of organizational breakdowns resulting from value conflicts and at the same time accounts for value conflicts that contribute to and build overall societal relations. Both of these conditions are evident in the 20th century method of organizing for inventiveness. Both conditions are accounted for in our development organization concepts.

The questions still remain: How do development organizations gain access to the resources of other systems? How do they secure the involvement of autonomous organized units without accepting the control of the resource allocators? At least two principles emerge as being relevant to these questions.

The first principle postulates that an organization will contribute resources and other organized efforts that will directly enhance the interests of the allocating organization. This principle represents a sufficient but not necessary condition for resource allocation involvement.

The second principle postulates that an organization will generally contribute resources to other organized efforts that will directly enhance the interest of a broader community of interests of which the allocating organization is a part. This principle also represents a sufficient but not necessary condition for resource allocation involvement.

When these two conditions are met we can postulate that it is impossible for any participant-recipient organization to deny the inherent character of a development organization project that has been defined as for the actual or potential good of the whole community of interests as well as for each member or group of that community. When such conditions are met, a development organization can gain access to resources of other systems without accepting control of the resource allocators.

A Development Organization

An illustration of the development organization theory in operation is the case of the Michigan Livestock Health Council. This section will relate the events leading up to formation of the council, describe its structure, and list its stated purpose and objectives.

No attempt is made to identify explicitly the corresponding theoretical development organization principles and constructs that form the bases of the events described. Rather, implicit recognition of and connections between the theoretical points and the case illustration are assumed by the author.

The Michigan Livestock Health Council

The Michigan Livestock Health Council was created by agricultural leaders of Michigan who recognized that the actions of organizations and their coalitions were of major importance in resolving ever-growing problems of agriculture. They understood that power for action, depends strongly upon the interorganizational linkages that exist between organized agricultural and nonagricultural interest groups.

The council formation thus reflects a significant change in the way in which agricultural resources are mobilized to solve complex agriculture problems. The basic notion of a statewide livestock health council tended to negate the traditional idea that agricultural power is located in the hands of independent producers whose base of authority and power is their area of specialization and their local community. Rather, a state council notion implicitly connotes the concept of an agricultural power formed and held by organizations of producers, processors, and varied service interests along commodity or special interest lines, lines that do not necessarily end at community, county, or even state boundaries, but reach out over the entire spectrum of activity and processes that carry the commodity from production to the consumer, through processing transportation, distribution, and consumption phases. This is a power spread that includes linkages into central complexes of education, business, industry, and government, many of them vast, and most extending far beyond community or county lines.

Initiation of the council idea came after completion of a very successful brucellosis eradication campaign in Michigan. A mayor key to the program's success had been the point effort of three interested groups—the Michigan Purebred Dairy Cattle Association, Cooperative Extension Service of Michigan State University, and the Michigan Department of Agriculture. The campaign generated such an interest in general programs of livestock health that the Department of Agriculture began to formulate plans for a general livestock health program in Michigan to be carried out through the cooperative efforts of the Michigan Purebred Dairy Cattle Association.

During the planning stages for this program, the director of the Michigan Department of Agriculture, the deans of Michigan State University's Colleges of Agriculture, Veterinary Medicine, and Home Economics, and the director of the MSU Extension Service met and discussed the livestock health problems in Michigan. After much consultation, the decision was made to abandon the agriculture department's plan to carry out a program through the Michigan Purebred Dairy Cattle Association in favor of an overall across-the-board cooperative approach that would investigate the entire area of livestock health research, education, regulation, and control in Michigan. This was to be a joint project of the Michigan Department of Agriculture and MSU, with the purpose of making a comprehensive effort to link the power of many organized interests in Michigan. The agency heads mentioned above then formed the administration policy group of the Michigan Livestock Health Council and went to work on improving livestock health for the good of the whole community of livestock interests in Michigan.

The IACD Committee

The first working phase of the new plan became the formation by the administration group of the Inter-Agency College Department committee (IACD), whose purpose was to systematically study the state's livestock health situation for all classes of livestock and make appropriate reports and recommendations to the administration policy group (Figure 10). This was a fact-finding group only.

The IACD was expected to get professional research people working together across disciplinary, agency, and departmental lines in order to make a comprehensive survey of the state of knowledge relative to livestock diseases in Michigan. The committee included three resource people from the Extension staff of MSU's College of Agriculture, and specialists in the production areas of poultry, swine, sheep, beef, and dairy husbandry. Extension personnel were included to provide a link with the field people and the producers out-state in order to feel the pulse and get their sentiments concerning livestock disease and health problems that faced them.

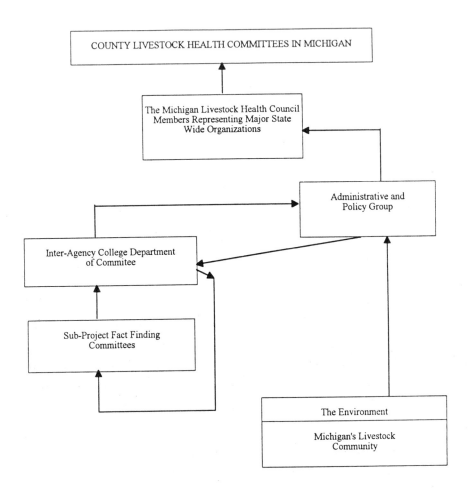

Figure 10.   *Relationship of the Inter-Agency College Department (IACD)
              committee to its environment*

Three representatives were selected from the College of Veterinary Medicine—a member of the Extension staff, a well-known expert on infectious diseases, and the head of the ambulatory service at Michigan State University who was particularly competent in the practicalities of applied veterinary medicine. Two representatives were chosen from the College of Home Economics, as it had been shown that farm women who work with home economic programs fill a critical role in implementing any farm action program and that knowledge channeled through them could have an impact upon an educational program of livestock health in Michigan.

The representative of the Michigan Department of Health brought with him a knowledge of the public health situation and a wealth of statistics concerning diseases of animals and humans and their transmission back and forth. The Department of Agriculture's representative was the Livestock Disease Control bureau chief, a man whose responsibilities included spearheading the state's livestock disease reporting service and acting as information coordinator between the control and ambulatory branches of the Livestock Disease Control Department in the agriculture department.

Representing the United States Department of Agriculture was the head of the tuberculosis and brucellosis project in Michigan. Michigan has conducted cooperative tuberculosis and brucellosis control programs with the federal government for years, and federal personnel have wide knowledge of and access to a variety of resources in federal disease control protects, especially in the fields of tuberculosis and brucellosis control and eradication.

The IACD committee, then, was made up of 11 representatives, and this became the core staff of the council for carrying out project work. Committee members were, in effect, temporarily transferred from their agencies to the Michigan Livestock Health Council. The function of the committee was to secure knowledgeable people who would serve on subcommittees to study livestock health problems in Michigan. A list of 40 livestock diseases causing problems in the state was compiled and 20 of these were selected for immediate consideration for either economic or humanitarian reasons. Reports of the subcommittees were filed with the IACD committee which set priorities for future study as well as determined criteria to be used in deciding priorities.

IACD Committee Report Format

One of the first jobs the IACD committee faced was determining what kind of a report they wanted to put out. A format for IACD reports was agreed upon and this format included:

* Importance of the disease in terms of—
  (a) public health
  (b) the state's economy

* Present status of the disease as related to such factors as—
  (a) its nature
  (b) its cause
  (c) how it is transmitted
  (d) its incidence
  (e) methods of control

* Recommendations for—
  (a) research
  (b) education (on and off campus)
  (c) regulation

* Action program recommendations in—
  (a) research (long- and short-term)
  (b) education
  (c) regulatory programs

* References

The IACD committee, acting as the actual heart of the council, formed a compact group so isolated that they could draw together resource people from all the sponsoring agencies and assign them specific tasks of studying and analyzing specific disease situations. IACD members were free to select whom they considered to be the best people available within the cooperating groups (USDA, Michigan Departments of Health and Agriculture, or any of the colleges at Michigan State University). They picked people on the basis of their knowledge rather than location or status. They expected a good, sound report from the assignee and it is felt that they generally got this. Difficulties were, of course, encountered. For example, a group appointed to study and report on a specific disease might bog down. In this case, the committee would set a deadline, go about their own work, and if, after a period of two or three months, the members were still inactive, would appoint a new committee to get the job done.

IACD Subcommittees

The subcommittees were appointed in the following manner: the IACD committee selected the subcommittee chairs who were then free to select their own committee members to conduct the study. The coordinator for IACD committee was thus not responsible for the details of council workers; he merely suggested names for the subcommittee chairs to draw on if they wished. The subcommittee chairs were free to work with people they wanted, and the IACD committee expended very little effort in personnel recruitment.

The working committees drew primarily on professional publications recognized as standards by members. The subcommittee design was helpful in securing information in that it enabled the IACD committee to cross department, college, and agency lines without becoming suspect. Although members reported they encountered some personality problems as they requested information on specific diseases, in general the committees worked very well.

The health council coordinator, who had experience working with large committees in the past, maintained that a big committee committed to a lot of things would "hit a snag" somewhere along the line, causing the whole project to blow up, taking up all the months and years of planning with it. The structuring of small independent subcommittees kept interest centered and growing around small specific problem areas. Then, as he put it, if a "small brush fire should break out in one of the subcommittees or its activities, it would be small enough to keep under control and not affect the rest of the larger group or endanger the entire project." At any rate, whether because of or in spite of this practice of using small and isolated working committees, the entire IACD project never was threatened.

The Council Proper

The administration policy group also commissioned a coordinator to help design an organizational structure that could be used to attack Michigan's livestock health problems. The task of the coordinator was to solicit the names of organizations of livestock producers, service interests, and others with interest in livestock or livestock products who would give sound active support to an overall state livestock health program. This task was accomplished with the assistance of the heads of several departments of MSU's colleges of agriculture, veterinary medicine, and home economics, plus Extension specialists from the same departments.

The organizations selected for council membership by this group were formally invited by a department head or an Extension specialist to participate in a formation meeting of the Michigan Livestock Health Council. In addition, other key influentials representing each of these organizations were invited personally by one of the Extension specialists to attend the formation meeting.

The meeting agenda, prepared by the coordinator, included statements by an administration policy group member that outlined the general concern about a specific livestock health program; these were backed up by supporting statements by department heads on the particular livestock health situation in their individual fields. A format of the proposed organization structure for the Michigan Livestock Health

Council was then presented. It included a list of objectives to be worked toward, a list of offices, with nominees, and an initial list of projects to be carried out by council subcommittees. A list of initial subcommittee appointments had also been compiled by the department heads and Extension specialists in the fields of dairy, poultry, animal husbandry, and veterinary medicine before the meeting, and this was presented.

The invitations were honored, the structural format was accepted, and the Michigan Livestock Health Council was born. The council was granted and accepted the authority and responsibility to be concerned with all livestock health problems in Michigan (Figure 11).

The Council's Operation

The council's activities were structured into three broad work areas: (1) research, (2) education, and (3) regulation. While its activities were primarily directed at in-state livestock health problems, the work today may carry interstate implications. The organizational structure was designed almost exclusively around the power component of influence rather than that of authority. That is, the council was not empowered to carry out its function through bureaucratic and hierarchical authoritarianism; rather, it could fulfill its objectives only on the basis of the influence it generated among the many resources it needed to achieve its goals. Its plan of operation includes an incorporation of:

* The involved action and obligations of many people and many interest groups on specific livestock health problems.

* The stimulation provided by research activity conducted in all areas of livestock health.

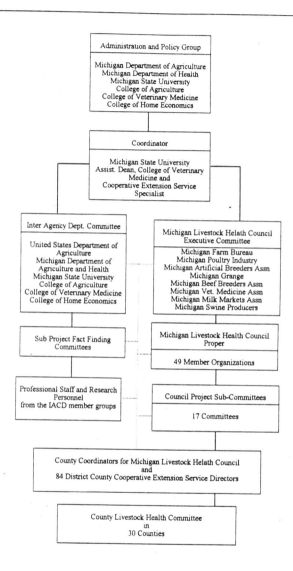

Figure 11.   *Organization chart of the Michigan Livestock Health Council*

*   The encouragement through dynamic efforts of effective legislative action relating to livestock health.

*   The effective regulation and observation of livestock health laws once they were established.

The council planned to achieve these goals by creating a climate of good will and deeds, so that help and resources would be forthcoming when needed. The council in turn would grow steadily in influence so that it could obtain ever-improved resources and greater help to better carry out its projects.

The objectives of the Michigan Livestock Health Council and the functions of the council, the executive committee, subcommittees, and advisory groups are formally stated as follows:

Michigan Livestock Health Council Objectives

*   Encourage a continuing evaluation of the livestock health situation in Michigan disease, diagnosis, reporting, and interpretation.

*   Encourage a continuing evaluation of the livestock health laws, regulations, and the enforcement of these statutes.

*   Provide guidance as to where emphasis should be placed in the livestock health programs

*   Provide liaison between Michigan's livestock owners and the various agencies that deal with livestock diseases.

*   Encourage the coordination of educational, research, and regulatory programs for livestock health.

*   Encourage and provide liaison within and between state and federal agencies.

* Provide liaison with professional associations concerned with the health of the livestock and people of Michigan.

The council meets at least two times each year to—

* Review the health situation of Michigan livestock and make recommendations regarding education, research, and regulatory programs in the area of livestock health.

* Assist in implementing specific livestock health programs.

* Receive progress reports and specific livestock health programs and recommend any necessary changes.

The executive committee was responsible for the achievement of the goals as established by the various committees and approved by the council. When a report approved by the council required changes in laws and regulations, additional funds, or additional personnel, this committee became active implementing such changes. The executive committee handled all business of the council while the council was not in session. The members of the advisory group were available for consultation with the council and the executive committee. The advisory group did not have voting privileges.

How the Council Worked

The history of the mastitis situation is provided here as an example of how a specific project was carried out.

* The subcommittee on mastitis presented a report to the IACD committee.

* IACD committee approved the report and sent it to the administration policy group.

* The administration policy group requested the head of MSU dairy department or his representative to submit the report to the Michigan Livestock Health Council.

* The chair of the council referred the report to the dairy members of the council for their recommendation, to be presented at the next council meeting.

* The dairy subcommittee report, which asked for changes in laws and regulations, additional funds and additional personnel, was referred to the executive committee for immediate action.

* The executive committee received progress reports on each recommendation made.

* The recommended programs were initiated as soon as possible, involving county groups, the Extension Service, the legislature, Michigan Department of Agriculture, and Michigan State University.

There is almost no way to justify and legitimize a council type of organization in the structure of most communities of interests. Basic to any organization must be a justifiable legitimate reason for its existence. For example, with respect to the council on livestock health, the following questions were pertinent: Is anyone or any organization responsible for overall planning of livestock health, research, education, and control? Does this person or group (informal or formal organization) possess the right to assume such responsibility? What body of citizens possesses the socially defined right to grant such a charter? What basis exists for legitimizing Michigan's Livestock Health Council activities? Is it possible to earn such a right of charter? Are livestock health problems of such a nature to justify a council type of organization for dealing with them? What livestock health problems can be met by a council-type organization that could not be solved in any other manner?

When the developments which led up to formation of the Michigan Livestock Health Council are examined closely, it becomes clear that among the prime ingredients were confusion, antagonism, and conflicts of philosophy, allegiance, and motivation, as well as feelings of good will and helpfulness. These differences occurred at all levels and revolved around such areas as agencies, departmental and personal philosophies, and boundaries. For it must be remembered that the basic concept of a livestock health council transcends, and generally negates, the individual autonomous values, both disciplinary and professional, of its constituent people and groups. As such, a council may easily represent a threat to, and in fact did threaten, many of the basic values that each of the participants strongly held. Of course, the council idea also offers an opportunity for member participants to achieve goals consistent with other such strongly held values.

The formation of such a council demands that some control of the resources of participating groups and organizations be transferred to the council itself. Organizational administrators recognize that this is a price they must pay in order to gain the benefits of a council. On the other hand, by relinquishing a certain amount of resource control, administrators also run the risk of having their agencies own resources used to thwart or alter certain objectives of their own organization.

This is a dilemma which, in the history of most council activity, is generally solved by the death of the council. Yet councils spring anew, for many problems of the day are like the problems of tuberculosis and brucellosis eradication. They transcend boundaries of species, localities, departments, agencies, and even philosophy. They demand that the questions listed above be answered affirmatively if effective action is ever to be taken. Such questions must be satisfactorily answered before socially correct legitimate justification can be claimed for the structuring and operation of a council type of development organization. In this case, the Michigan Livestock Health Council did provide innovative solutions to important disease problems that had caused its formation in the first place. In the end, however, the initial sponsors of this development organization withdrew their support and the council withered away.

Chapter 9

A TECHNIQUE FOR PREDICTING
INTRAORGANIZATIONAL ACTION[1]

*Knowledge is an image, it is what is believed to be
true and as such it governs behavior. The most
fundamental proposition is that knowledge is what
somebody or something knows, and that without a
knower, knowledge is an absurdity* (Boulding, 1961).

To predict the results of organizational action requires analytic
techniques that, when fitted to appropriate theory, can quickly and
efficiently seek out and measure crucial variables that offer understandable and reliable explanations of intraorganizational action. Many
theorists have proposed models to explain intraorganizational action,
most of which do provide guidelines for predicting the consequences of
such action. Prediction, however, requires empirical data and tools,

---

[1]This work first appeared in *Clinical Sociology Review* Vol. 8, 1990. It is printed
here with the Journal's permission.

which we generally do not have. There is the need to forge a closer link between the theoretical and empirical analyses of organizations.

In this chapter, I have attempted to describe an analytical technique that can, for a given organization, quickly, accurately, and efficiently transform abstract theoretical propositions into concrete empirical indices. The problem as stated calls for the development of an analytical technique and instrument that will systematically put basic theoretical concepts into an operational form.

In order to do this, it was first necessary to determine what important or limiting factors are related to intraorganizational analysis. A search of the literature reveals some common threads that are generally recognized by all organizational theorists.

First, it was quite clear that perceptions of an organization itself vary. Not only do views of an organization change with time, but the characteristic properties included in the many perceptions held about an organization tend to vary with the position from which the view was taken. Was the organization perceived from the public view? From the internal organizational view? From the view of an impartial analyst? Or from the view of a person occupying a position within that organization?

The analyst of an organization is thus presented with the dilemma of determining whose view, or what view, accurately depicts the crucial aspects of the organization's operation. Regardless of the accuracy or validity of the various views or images held concerning the organization, however, these views do affect the operation of the organization.

This leads us directly to the second dilemma. By what criteria can the many views be measured and weighed? How do we determine the relative importance of these many views for any given organization?

Some theorists maintain that answers to these questions can be obtained by using rational techniques. They argue that, because an organization is a rationally conceived creation of humans, it can be analyzed on the basis of measurements taken from its formal patterns of operation. Other theorists argue that it is not enough just to measure or manipulate the formally described elements of an organization. They contend that an organization also must deal with its external environment, which is not always rational in design. For them, measures that tend to emphasize the organization's equilibrium and how this equilibrium is maintained become an appropriate analytic form.

Yet another concern of theorists is the level at which these measurements are taken. Should they be taken at the survival or sheer maintenance level of organizational operation, at the point of most effective operation, or at the point of efficient resource maximization?

All theorists ultimately face the question of measuring, or at least dealing with, a specific organization's goals and subgoals. The problem again becomes one of choice—whose goals, or what goals, are to be dealt with, and at what level of achievement are they to be measured or evaluated?

These are but a few of the problems, admittedly oversimplified, that are faced and by those who would theorize about, or analyze, organizations. The solutions to these many problems must finally be measured against the value system selected as a standard in the analysis. Will it be (1) the value system of the organization's members, (2) the value system of the organization's resource-input system, (3) the value system of its product-user system, (4) the value system of total society, or (5) perhaps all of these and more?

It is sufficient to say that nearly overwhelming difficulties beset any organization analyst from the start. For even if a satisfactory method were available for dealing with these problems, no doubt the simple things such as the availability of a researcher's time and the physical resources available to an analyst are important limitations that would soon become the major limiting factors to a meaningful detailed analysis of any specific organization.

The technique presented here represents a synthesis of features from three organizational models—the *rational, natural system,* and *effectiveness* models—with certain concepts taken from a fourth, the *perceptual* model (Bartley 1958; March and Simon 1959; Snygg and Combs 1949). This technique attempts to satisfy Gouldner's (1959) plea for a resynthesis of the rational and natural system models. It is also compatible with Etzioni's (1960) suggestion that the "system model," with its view of the social unit as a process and its insistence on examination of the external and internal conditions that enable it to function, is the most appropriate means of studying organizations. This technique attempts to fulfill the scientific purposes of description, explanation, and prediction (Hempel and Oppenheim 1953) of an organization's efficiency in achieving its goals.

Characteristics of Organizational Systems

An organization is an artifact. It is a social group; but unlike a natural society, it has been assembled to serve a purpose. It is a bureaucratically arranged social group with at least one specifiable goal (Simon 1964). That is, its members have differentiated functions that relate to a goal of the organization (an organizational goal is a state of affairs for which the organization exists to bring into being, an image of a future state which may or may not be brought about). Once a goal is achieved, it becomes a part of the organization or of its environment and is thus no longer an image guiding organizational activities, and no longer a goal (Etzioni 1961).

A system is considered to be a conventionally selected set of variables that interact. These variables are defined in such a way that, given the state of the system at specified time intervals, its state at any other given time can be predicted. This set of interacting variables may be (and doubtless will be) a subset of a larger set of variables. In other words, the system to be studied may be a part of a larger system.

The elements of a system are the entities of the system that reflect its substantive content. They are the descriptive terms of the system. *Variables* of a system are the conditions of these elements within an organization at given times. The values of the variables at any given time define the state of the system at that time. They carry the implications of change or variation regardless of the precision with which this change can be measured.

Parameters of the system are the condition of elements outside the organization that act upon and interact with it as environmental variables. Both the internal organizational variables and the parameters, or external organizational variables, have a wide range of effects on an organization. To induce change, one must determine those variables that are significant to the functioning of the organized system, for change in an organization occurs through change in either or both the variables or the parameters of a system.

In selecting the elements to include in an analysis of an organizational system, the theorist (Andrew 1961) ultimately asks this basic question: Should the element or variables to be used in analyzing a system be selected by *a priori* logic or through successive empirical testing methods? Parsons (1956), for example, attempts to identify the constituent elements and their relationships in a total social systems model. For Parsons, organizations are total social systems with primary orientations toward the attainment of specific goals. With this concept, Parsons assumes that the parts are interdependent. Merton (1957), in his concern for the degree of interdependency of organizational parts, attempts to select elements of a system on the basis of empirical determination. Gouldner (1959) sees the selection of elements as a cumulative process through which a battery of explanatory variables will be sifted out by empirical observation. He states unequivocally that the inclusion or exclusion of elements in the social system is not susceptible to "purely theoretical resolution." He points out that "problematic patterns" can only be partially explained on an empirical basis because only a partial knowledge of the constituent element of a social system can be obtained with empirical accumulation techniques. It would not be possible, therefore, to relate those patterns to the system as a whole.

It is clear that when the selection of elements is made, some important element or variable may be left out because the process of selection is arbitrary. Consequently, the methods of both *a priori* and empirically tested selection are necessary. The determination of what elements to include falls into the context of discovery, while empirical testing for accuracy of the selection falls into the context of validation.

No satisfactory means has yet been developed to systematically take into account the significance of variation in the degree of interdependence of selected elements, because they are parts of an "open system." Thus, the patterns of behavior can be only partially explained for a given period of time, for all systems have an infinite set of properties. In this methodology, it is suggested that variables will account for the relationships of the internal system elements selected, and the parameters may account for environmental change. The external factors, parameters or environmental, should be reflected, at least in part, by the perception of position incumbents of the system under analysis.

This methodology suggests an approach that attempts to resolve both the question of element selection and the question of degree of variation, or interrelatedness, of these elements. Note that the schema outlined calls for identification and selection of the elements of the organization to be analyzed by the members of that organization. This is accomplished by use of the "Open-ended Question" (OEQ) device. Variation in the interrelatedness of these elements is also measured by the organization's members, by their scalings on an instrument called the "Rating Scale" (RS) device.

The Theory to Be Used

Within this framework, it is now possible to fit a theory to the analytic technique. The theoretical organization concepts developed by Sower (Sower et al. 1962; Sower, 1962) are used as the substantive theory fitted to the analytical methods and tools described in this chapter. It should be clear from the outset that the technique described can be fitted with a wide range of theoretical substantive variables. The technique and instruments described provide the means for transcribing these theoretical variables into concrete empirical, analytical forms. The major assumptions of Sower's theory are—

*   The key to understanding and explaining the operations of an organization and their consequences is the organizational link between its subgroups.

*   The extent to which an organization achieves its goals is a consequence of certain internal variables. These variables are subject to change upon decisions of persons who occupy specific positions in the organization. A corollary of this assumption is that these variables, when identified, are capable of being described and explained and the relationships between them predicted.

*   The actions of the incumbent of a position within an organization will agree with his/her own expectations of behavior proper to that position and what he/she perceives the expectations of relevant others to be, whether they are shared by a majority or not, and whether or not his/her perceptions are accurate.

The relationships between the organizational variables are explained by Sower's *Model for Explaining and Predicting the Relationships between Internal Organizational Variables and the Extent of Goal Achievement for a Development Organization.* Briefly, this model accounts for the following internal relationships:

* The extent to which the organization's members have clearly defined conception of its purpose or goal

* The extent to which the organization imposes upon its members patterns of expected behavior that are congruent with their own behavior expectations

* The extent to which the organization's members are interested in achieving its goals

These relationships are the intervening variables of the model; consensus among members of the organization on each variable selected directly determines the extent to which the organization is likely to achieve its goal. Postulates constructed from these three intervening variables may be expressed as follows:

Postulate I:
The degree to which an organization will achieve its goal is directly related to the extent to which its members have a clear conception of the organization's purpose or goal.

The general predictive formula expressing this relationship is:

⁰OGA f ⁰COG$_m$ when ⁰OGA = the degree of organization's goal achievement and ⁰COG$_m$ = the degree of clarity of members' conception of organization's purpose or goal.[2]

Postulate II:

The degree to which an organization will achieve its goal is directly related to the extent to which the organization imposes on its members patterns of expected behavior that are congruent with their own behavioral expectations.

The general predictive formula expressing this relationship is:

⁰OGA f ⁰CBE$_m$ when ⁰OGA = the degree of organization's goal achievement and ⁰CBE$_m$ = the degree to which members have behavioral expectations congruent with that of the organization.

Postulate III:

The degree to which an organization will achieve its goal is directly related to the extent to which its members are interested in achieving the goal.

The formula expressing this relationship is:

⁰OGA f ⁰IOG$_m$ when ⁰OGA = the degree of organization's goal achievement and ⁰IOG$_m$ = the extent to which position incumbents, or organizations' members, are interested in achieving the goals of that organization.

---

[2] The symbol f represents the phrase, "is directly related to," and will be used in this sense throughout this chapter. Note that Sowers' constructs call only for the perceptions of organization members. These are called *variables of the system*. The subscript "m" in the formula expresses this limitation. If the theory used calls for perception of external "relevant others" who are not formal members of the organization—*parameter of the system*—as well as member perceptions, the technique will accommodate such a formulation. This would be expressed in Postulate I by use of the subscript "o," in the following manner ⁰OGA f ⁰COG$_m$ f ⁰COG$_o$.

Population and Sampling Procedures

The population is defined as all members of the organization to be studied. In studies of organizations with relatively few members (100 or less), the total population may be included in the sample. In studies of large organizations (over 100), a stratified random sample of respondents of an appropriate but manageable size should be drawn as outlined by Kish (1953). The stratification criterion may be the hierarchical division already existing in the organization. Other criteria also may be specified. Random samples of respondents should be drawn from each stratum.

Element Identification and Measurement

The subcategories (or elements) that make up the independent variables are determined by an Open-ended Question (OEQ) device (see Figure 12) constructed along the lines of the 20-Statement Problem (Kuhn and MacPortland 1954). This device is administered to respondents at all levels of the organizational hierarchy. The OEQ device asks respondents to express their personal notions about each of the three independent variables derived from the three postulates listed above. Responses to the OEQ device are categorized and reworded to form an RS device, which is then administered to respondents for scaling. Data derived from the RS device form the basic interval scale data used in statistical manipulations. Scale data were used to determine the degree of consensus and rank-ordered differences in the perceived expectations of the different respondents toward the three major intervening consensus factors selected for analysis.

The Michigan Livestock Health Council is now 1 ½ years old.
A.   What do you believe to be the purpose of the ... Council?
      1.
      2.
      n.

B.   In your opinion, what do others who are interested
      in livestock and livestock products now think the
      purpose of the ... Council to be?
      1.
      2.
      n.

C.   In your opinion, what are the most impor-
      tant specific projects that the ... Council
      has engaged in?
      1.
      2.
      n.

D.   In your opinion what specific projects
      should be acted upon by the ... Council?
      1.
      2.
      n.

Figure 12.   *A sample of the Open-ended Question device (OEQ)*

The Open-Ended Question (OEQ) Device

The Open-ended Question device is a relatively unstructured
instrument that attempts to determine the concept of the purpose or
goal of an organization as seen by its members. The OEQ device consists
of one question per single page, followed by blank spaces in which

respondents are asked to answer the question. The OEQ device is a self-administered paper-and-pencil test; it can be administered directly to respondents or indirectly by mail.

The questions are derived from the theoretical postulates used in the analysis. For example, questions derived from Postulate I as used in a research setting are reproduced in Figure 12 (Anderson 1963). The following assumptions underlie use of the OEQ device:

* The internal conception of an organization is related to the way members of the organization act and how they identify themselves in relationship to the actions and identities attributed to them by others who hold authoritative positions and who ascribe roles. The self-conception of an organization is formed from the experience of its members. This self-concept and self-expectation of members lead to an organizational self-concept and self-expectation that guides the organization's ongoing social behavior. Consequently, these self-expectations of the organization have predictive utility.

* The important elements of an organization's self-conception are accessible and indexable at the awareness level through member statements. The statements about an organization solicited from its members provide a direct approach to the organization's self-concept. When members are confronted with the problem of identifying the organization they belong to, they must decide for themselves how this identification will be made. They do so as socialized members of the organization and society at large. Therefore members tend to reflect the normative expectation and behavior patterns that specifically characterize that organization.

Obviously, an infinite number of descriptive statements could be made by members about their organization. Consequently, the OEQ device accounts for a very small fraction of all possible elements of descriptive statements that respondents might make.

Research utilizing the similar 20-Statement Problem (Kuhn and MacPortland 1954) indicates that even a small sample of statements about the self is useful, since it permits stable differentiation among persons and reliable predictions about their behavior. It is held, then, that an analytic transfer of self-concept from an individual to an organization can be made without a significant loss in the reliability or predictive usefulness of the 20-Statement Problem methodology, or in this case, the equivalent OEQ device.

Administration of the OEQ Device

As mentioned, respondents (organizational members) to the OEQ device may be gathered in groups (conference setting) or dealt with individually, either directly or by mail. In any setting, respondents must be given an acceptable reason for responding. Reasons will vary with circumstances, but respondents must be assured that (1) they are free to express their deep concerns about the organization, (2) these concerns will be carefully considered in future decision-making actions of the organization, and (3) no personal punishment or reward will be forthcoming as a result of wholehearted participation in the analysis.

In order to preserve the unstructured nature of the OEQ device, it is important to give no indication of possible or expected responses either before or during the administration. The device should be self-administered and should require no additional explanation by those administering it. Any questions raised should be answered with vague generalities (examples: "anything you want to put down," "whatever you think," "yes, that is fine," or "yes, that's the sort of thing").

The quality of responses is likely to vary inversely with the amount of time allowed for the administration of this device. A number of factors, such as interest, fatigue, etc., contribute to this phenomenon. It is recommended that a maximum time limit of 15 minutes per question be set. When indirect administrations are employed, a time limit might be suggested on the query sheet, even though it is impossible to enforce compliance uniformly. In conference settings, respondents who complete their answers in less than the allotted time should be free to leave if they so desire.

It is desirable, for control purposes, to secure both the respondent's organizational position and signature on the OEQ device. Respondents should be assured that no superordinate or subordinate personnel in the organization will have access to their responses.

Analysis and Classification of Responses

Information gathered from the OEQ device alone provides a sound base for both qualitative and quantitative analysis of the researched organization. At least three different analytical forms can be employed: an analysis of literal content (an analysis of a level of meaningfulness to the respondents themselves); a more abstract analysis of referential frames; and, perhaps the most abstract, the logical form into which statements made by the respondents arranged themselves.

However, my technique does not attempt to use the information obtained by this device in any direct analytical form. Rather, the OEQ device is used for the sole purpose of generating and selecting significant elements or description statements about the organization. These statements are then numbered and classified as to their literal content by using *subject* as one criterion and *action verb* as a second classification criterion.

Once the range of subjects and the degree of action imputed to these subjects have been classified, a representative sample of the entire range of classified responses is formed into a Rating Scale device. This final device contains, initially, the *elements* of the organization to be analyzed. These elements are now in the form of literal and highly specific descriptive statements about the organization.

The Rating Scale (RS) Device

The interpretation of the results obtained from the Rating Scale device will be based on the notion of consensus or variation of the elements as perceived by members of the organization under analysis. Here I, as did Gross et al. (1958), treat consensus as a *variable* rather than as an attribute. In this framework, the complete presence and complete absence of consensus are limiting cases. The first rarely, if ever, occurs in social action; the second occurs frequently, but not inevitably.

Considering consensus on role definition to be a variable brings up the following questions: How much and on what aspects is consensus essential to the effective functioning of an organization? Are there optimum degrees of consensus? Are extreme degrees of consensus dysfunctional? How little consensus can there be without the disintegration of the organization?

To investigate consensus problems empirically, it is necessary first to specify the organization, its objects, and the member populations to be analyzed; and second, to obtain data on the expectations held for and by members concerning specific variables. A methodology based on "consensus" must specify clearly "consensus on what" and "consensus among whom" (Gross et al. 1958).

In the methodology developed for this technique, the degree of consensus measured refers to the elements or descriptive statements about the organization as perceived by its members. These elements were derived from the three intervening variable postulates specified by Sower's theory. The specific formulation of the element was accomplished through the use of the OEQ device. The Rating Scale (RS) device asks each member to what extent he or she agrees with the elements (specific descriptive statements) as stated. The respondent chooses one of the following response categories for each element: (1) strongly agree, (2) agree, (3) may or may not agree, (4) disagree, or (5) strongly disagree. Sample questions derived from Postulate 1, which were used in the Livestock Health Council Study, are presented in Figure 13.

The purpose of the Michigan Livestock Health Council should be to—
(Rating Scale: 1 = Strongly agree → 5 = Strongly disagree)

1 2 3 4 5   1.   Provide the means for various interest groups
                       to communicate and work together in solving
                       or trying to solve livestock and poultry disease
                       problems.

1 2 3 4 5   2.   Continually review and evaluate the livestock
                       and poultry health situation in Michigan.

1 2 3 4 5   3.   Develop and coordinate cooperative programs
                       of disease eradication in livestock and poultry
                       between producers, processors, consumers,
                       and other interest groups.

1 2 3 4 5   4.   Promote initially and back those laws regulating
                       programs which are essential and practical to
                       safeguard the health of Michigan's livestock
                       and poultry.

Figure 13.   *A sample Rating Scale (RS) device*

Given a series of distributions, each of which is comprised of the responses to a single expectation item containing the five response categories, the problem is obtaining scores that will rank the items on a continuum of consensus. Gross et al. (1958) point out that if all responses for an item fall in one category, there is perfect consensus. However, not all will approach or even come near this extreme. Consequently, two factors—central tendencies and variability and the distribution—need to be considered in consensus measurements. These statistics should account for both the score and the range of scored distributions obtained.

Results of earlier research appear to bear out this supposition. Gross et al. (1958) found that mean and variance satisfactorily reflect degree measurements of consensus; measures of central tendency such as mean, mode, or median, in calling attention to direction of the measurements taken, give similar results. The use of variance scores of the distribution was found to offer the advantage over other distribution statistics by calling attention to disagreements on intensity rather than on direction. That is, the responses given could be all positive or all negative and still present meaningful differences.

The use of variance as a statistic lends itself easily to a variety of statistical computations and manipulations. For example, the difference in the degree of consensus on a given element for the various subgroups of the selected organization can be quickly determined by the F test, variance ratio, chi-square, or other easily applied statistical tests.

The interpretation of the findings obtained from the RS device is therefore based on the variance of the grand mean score or mean score of all respondents as the defined *measure of consensus.* A small variance is defined as consensus; a large variance is defined as no consensus. It is arbitrarily held that any variation about the grand mean score equal to or greater than 1 standard deviation from the mean variation, or any variance equal to or greater than 1 at the probable a.95 level of significance, is, by definition, a significant difference in variation and, therefore, does not meet the test for consensus.

In this procedure, the statistical test used to determine the difference in variance at any specified level of significance is the One-Sided Test of Hypothesis concerning a Single Variance (Nixon and Massey 1957). The hypothesis tested is $\sigma^2 \leq \sigma^2$. If the level of significance selected is $a.95$, the statistic is $x^2/df = (s^2/\sigma^2_0) \, \sigma^2 \leq \sigma^2_0$.

Summary

Analytical instruments applicable for use in the analysis of complex organizations must be tight, reliable, and efficient tools that are economical and easy to use. At the same time, these instruments should be flexible enough to allow respondents to express themselves freely and concisely. Among other things, the technique and instruments described, when fitted with an appropriate theory, feature:

* **Open-ness**—that is, this technique approaches the specific organization in its initial contact with a relatively unstructured Open-ended Question device. The purpose of the device is to permit respondents (members of the organization) to identify and select elements of their organization that they perceive as important to that organization. The OEQ device thus represents an alternative solution to the basic problem of choice faced by the organizational analyst when attempting to determine what and whose view about what and whose goals to include in the research.

* **Closed-ness**—that is, with its follow-up device, the Rating Scale, this technique ultimately forces respondents to provide scaled measurements of consensus variations about specific elements that comprise the intervening test variables. Note that the scaled responses are generated from the organization's members.

* **Self-ness**—that is, the analysis is conducted from within the organization itself as reflected through the perceptions of its members. It is an analysis of the organization "self."

* **Efficiency**—that is, the technique and its instrumentation are designed to minimize time, physical resources, and costs of obtaining an optimum amount of descriptive explanatory and predictive information about a specific organization. By using this technique and its instrumentation, it is possible for an outside researcher or consultant to enter a complex organization and, within a matter of a few days' time, objectively describe and make predictive probability statements concerning that organization's patterns of intraorganizational action.

Chapter 10

A SOCIOMETRIC APPROACH
TO THE ANALYSIS OF
INTERORGANIZATIONAL RELATIONSHIPS[1]

Today's experimentalists, as did the philosopher Plato in ancient Greece, are searching for truth by asking questions like What are the limits of human knowledge? Is the world shaped in some sense by our perception of it? Is there an element of randomness in the universe or are all events predetermined? (Horgan 1992).

Despite our recognition of the interdependence of organizations, it is rare to find sociological research that deeply penetrates interorganizational phenomena (Evan 1966; Etzioni 1964; March 1965). Recognizing this deficiency, a group of social scientists at Michigan State University have attempted to explore this sketchily charted field. Our primary objective was to develop a methodological approach for use in

[1]This work first appeared in *Inter-Organizational Relations*, 1976. It is printed here with the publisher's permission.

the study of the interorganizational relationships of a community or region. The specific concern was an examination of these relationships as they bear on the process of area development.

Our work, in this particular context, is based in large part on the following postulates:

* Social power is structured.

* The social structure of a region is made up of constellations of interdependent heterogeneous interacting organizations. These represent basic resource holding, allocating, and receiving units.

* The organizations within a region have a fabric of roles that constitute the social organization of that region. Within this structure, individual organizations act and contribute in accordance with role prescriptions or expectations. They perform and coordinate their activities with one another in accordance with the relationship of their own roles to other roles in the structure.

* Organizations are the basic units of power.

* Organizations represent the basic social units responsible for development. Societal development is carried out by some combination of large, small, simple, complex, public, or private organizations.

* Organizations are in themselves basic resources of development activity, as are air, water, iron, trees, etc.

* Organizations are control mechanisms by means of which power for development is generated and through which it flows.

    *   Organizations cannot exist in isolation; every organization is related to a cluster of interdependent organizations.

    *   Organizations form constellations in order to achieve development goals. As specific issues arise, overlapping constellations of special-interest organizations are formed. A specific organization sometimes cooperates, at other times competes, and at still other times is not involved with other organizations in issue resolution.

    *   A given organization's involvement and influence in issue resolution and/or in development depend upon the place it occupies in the legitimate order of the organized constellation of organizations affected by the issue and or the developmental activity. For any given issue, some organizations are more powerful than others. An organization's "power rank" will generally vary with the issue to be resolved.

With the development of sociometric techniques, it was almost inevitable that these procedures would be used in the study of power and influence in community. However, sociometric techniques generally have not been used to analyze interorganizational relationships. In effect, ours is an exploratory attempt to transpose what traditionally has been a small group, interpersonal approach to a large-scale, interorganizational setting.

    Two specific methodologies heavily influenced the design of this sociometric approach. The first was Hunter's nomination-reputational method of social analysis. Using a modified version of this technique, we produced an organizational inventory profile of the perceived organized structure of Michigan's Upper Peninsula. The universe of organizations to be included in the sociometric analysis was drawn from this inventory. Secondly, Weiss and Jacobson's (1955) set of structured concepts and methodology demonstrated the feasibility of using sociometric analysis in the study of complex structures. While Weiss and Jacobson have done as much as anyone to develop and promote the use of the sociometric approach in the analysis of complex organizations, they do not extend such use beyond intraorganizational activity. The success of sociometric techniques in small group research and Weiss and Jacobson's imaginative use of them in analyzing the structure of complex organizations led us to believe that sociometric techniques would provide a useful means of gaining information at the interorganizational level. In our transposition of traditional sociometric techniques (Gardner and Byrne 1968), we obtained sociometric measures indicating dependency ties among an identified universe of organizations, as perceived and recorded by responsible organization members empowered by each organization to speak for their respective organizations. The sociometric choices were made in terms of particular criteria and the data obtained provided *degree-of-dependency* information relating to three interorganizational variables: (I) interaction structures, (2) influence patterns, and (3) status arrangements.

Application of the Approach to Economic Development of a Region

A case study is presented here to illustrate the methodological aspects of our approach. The specific goal of the case study was to identify organizations responsible for economic development in

Michigan's 15-county Upper Peninsula region, and to discover the dependence relationships existing among them. Organizations included were those that could significantly affect economic development activity in the region by taking one of three alternative courses of action:

* Becoming actively involved and committing resources to a given development project.

* Maintaining a neutral position in regard to a given development project, but in so doing acting as a potential influence in either support or opposition to the project.

* Becoming actively involved and committing resources in opposition to a given development project.

On the basis of a review of existing economic reports and records on the Upper Peninsula, 11 major economic-interest sectors were identified and selected for study: forestry, mining, tourism, agriculture, business, manufacturing, fishing, utilities, transportation, communications, and government service. It was our belief that each organization identified would be involved in continuing relations with certain others, and that the networks of interdependence would tend to enclose distinct clusters of heterogeneous organizations. We assumed that—

* The resources for development in a region are mobilized and controlled mainly by organizations.

* One organization's actions have a strong impact on others in a related cluster and lesser impact outside of the cluster.

* Decisions affecting the development of the region are not made alone by the inner councils of management in each

organization, but by a process that admits the influence of other organizations.

Knowledge of the dependency patterns among organizations is thus viewed as an important aspect of the economic planning and development of a region.

Universe Selection

An interview schedule was designed allowing for open-ended nominations of organizations having a legitimate special interest in one or more of the 11 interest sector categories. Key informants—persons holding formal and operational positions in specific organizations in each of the selected interest sectors—nominated organizations they considered to be the significant units controlling the economic development activities in 11 economic-interest sectors of Michigan's Upper Peninsula. The data were collected on a county basis and data obtained from the interviews were considered to be additive. Thus, as new organizations were nominated, they were added to the inventory list of nominated organizations until no new organizations were obtained and only the frequency of nominations increased. This treatment of the data tends to correct for the bias introduced by the selective sampling procedure used. The result obtained is a comprehensive Warren-type (1972) horizontal and vertical, two-dimensional inventory of organizations. A sample illustration of the nature of the data obtained for the transportation interest sector is presented in Figure 14.

In order to obtain a manageable universe of organizations for the sociometric analysis phase of the study, only those organizations receiving multiple nominations were included. Universe reduction using the multiple-nominations criterion meant that only organizations receiving two or more nominations (1) within and/or between counties, and (2) within and/or between interest sectors were to be included in the study.

The horizontal dimension represents the number of organizations nominated within each county. Note that only one transportation-related organization was nominated in Ontonagon County, while six were nominated in Chippewa County. Ontonagon County exhibits a monolithic, simple horizontal transportation structure while Chippewa County exhibits a more pluralistic, complex horizontal structure.

The vertical dimension is represented by the recognized extra-county or regional scope of activity of a given organization. Clairmont Transfer, Greyhound Bus, and Olson Transportation Company all clearly exhibit extensive extra-county or vertical influence in the Upper Peninsula transportation sector, while Moland Brothers Trucking Company, Buccanero Transfer Company, Northwestern Motor Bus Company, etc., exhibit restrictive and highly localized activity patterns.

The data as presented in Figure 14 do not, however, provide much insight into the real or potential power or influence of any individual organization in relation to all others. They do not tell us anything about how these organizations interact with one another. We attempted to obtain answers about these and other factors by use of a sociometric technique.

Organized Interests \ Counties	Houghton-Keweenaw	Ontonagon	Gogebic	Iron	Baraga	Marquette	Dickinson	Menominee	Delta	Schoolcraft	Alger	Luce	Chippewa	Mackinaw
Claimont Transfer Co.	*	**	••	••	••	••	••	••	••		••	••	••	
Automobile Dealer Assn.	•	•												
Greyhound Bus Co.	•		•	••	••	•			•			•	••	
Moland Bors. Trucking Co.			••											
Buccanero Transfer Co.			•											
Northwestern Motor Bus Co.			•											
Wisc.-MI Transit Co.				•										
Olson Transportation Co.					•	••	••	••	••		••			
Allied Van Lines					•									
Nystrom's Moving & Storage					•									
Freeman Trucking					•									
Stang Tank Line						•								
Anderson Motor Service						•								
McNeal Ford Sales						•								
Teamster's Union								•						••
Michigan Trucker's Assn.								•						
Swanson Trucking Co.										•				
Ameon Transfer Co.										•				•
US Mail Limousine										•				
Bray Taxi										•				
Knauf Chevrolet											•			
Chippewa Co. Road Comm.													•	
Short Transfer Co.													•	
Lock City Trans. Co.													•	
North Star Bus Co.													•	

Figure 14.   *The perceived organized structure of the transportation interest sector of Michigan's Upper Peninsula by county*

Sociometric Instrumentation

To measure interorganization interaction, organizational officials, representing each organization included in the analysis, were asked to check the appropriate (*frequently, occasionally, never*) cell in order to rate the relationship of their organization with every other organization in the study (see Figure 15). Each rating referred to a discrete point on a high-low (3-2-l) continuum reflecting frequency or intensity of interaction.

Sociometric Analysis of Interorganizational Data

Once the sociometric data are obtained, it is possible to carry out a number of analytic procedures that will yield useful information about interorganizational relationships.

We calculated sociometric scores, ranked scores given/received by each organization in relation to every other one, and defined and computed sociometric scores for each of the $\underline{n}$ organizations as the average squared frequency of the interaction score given to (or received by) the $\underline{ith}$ organization by the remaining n-1 organizations in the universe.

Figure 16 lists the organizations included in the analysis by rank order of sociometric scores received from and given to all other organizations. High scores indicate high interorganizational dependency; low scores indicate low interorganization dependency. The sociometric scores received data are derived from a sufficiently large number of organizational sources to allow for interorganizational generalization. The sociometric scores given data, on the other hand, are generated from single organizational sources and consequently do not allow for such generalization but are useful indicators of individual organizational dependency.

Sociometric scores **received** by each organization from all other organizations in the study indicate other organizational dependency upon that organization. For example, city and village government received a relatively high average sociometric score (6.46) from other organizations (Figure 16), which we interpret to mean that the organizations included in the study tend to be highly dependent upon city and village government in their normal business activities. The Teamsters' Union, on the other hand, received a very low sociometric score (1.80), indicating that the organizations in the study did not express much dependency on the union in the execution of their normal business activities.

Sociometric scores **given** by each organization to all other organizations in the study indicate that organization's dependence upon the other organizations. Figure 16 shows that the Escanaba Daily Press gave all other organizations a high average sociometric score of 7.19. This is interpreted to mean that the Daily Press is highly dependent upon the organizations included in the study in carrying out its normal newspaper activities. The U.P. Law Enforcement Association gave other organizations a low average score of 2.07, indicating that the LEA has a low dependency relationship with the other organizations in the study. These data provide the researcher with a large bank of raw information concerning the dependency patterns of all organizations in the analysis.

ORGANIZATION	3	2	1	ORGANIZATION	3	2	1
Abbott Fox Lumber Co.				Mead			
Agr. Stabilization Comm. USDA				Mich. Artificial Breeders Assn.			
Ahonen Land & Lumber Co.				Michigan Bell			
American Can Corp.				Michigan Education Assn.			
Area Redevelopment Admin.				Milwaukee Road RR Co.			
Barrett Lumber Co.				Michigan State University			
Boards of Supervisors (Co.)				Michigan Technical University			
Bur. of Commercial Fisheries				Mich & Wisc Timber Products			
Calumet & Hecla, Inc.				Nat'l Park Service (US Dept)			
Celotex Corp.				North Central Airlines			
Chambers of Commerce (City)				North Range Mining Co.			
Chicago and N.W. RR Co.				Northern Michigan University			
City & Village Government				Ontonagon Valley REA Power			
CJIC TV Sault Ste. Marie				Operation Action U.P.			
Clairmont Transfer Co.				Paper Makers & Workers AFL			
Cleveland Cliffs Iron Co.				Pettibone Mich. Corp. (Baraga)			
Cliffs-Dow Chemical Co.				Pickands-Mather Mining Co.			
Cloverland REA				Planning Comm. (City & Vill.)			
Congress (US)				Planning Comm. (County)			
Conner Lumber & Land Co.				Potato Growers Assn. (U.P.)			
Conservation Dept. (MI)				Public Schools			
Coop. Ext. Service (MSU)				Republican Party (County)			
Copper Range Co.				Road Commission (County)			
County Dairy Herd Imp. Assn.				Sawyer-Stoll			
Democratic Party (County)				Sheriff (County)			
Detroit Edison				Soil Conserv. Service (USDA)			
Drummond Dolomite Inc.				Soo Line			
Econ. Expansion Comm. (MI)				State Police (MI)			
Edison Sault Power Co.				Supt. of Schools (County)			
Escanaba Daily Press				Superior Studs, Inc.			
Forest Service (USDA)				Teamsters' Union			
F.P. Furlong Co.				The Daily Mining Gazette			
FORUM				The Evening News			
General Telephone				The Mining Journal			
GOINC (Gogebic)				UPCAP			
Goodman & Mohawk Lumber				U.P. Law Enforcement Assn.			
Huss Ontonagon Pulp & Paper				U.P. Power Co.			
Inland Lime and Stone Co.				U.P. Tourist Assn.			
Inland Steel Co.				US Army Corps of Engineers			
Iron Mt. News				United Steel Workers AFL-CIO			
Keweenaw Land Assn. Ltd.				University of Michigan			
Kimberly Clark of Michigan				WDBC Radio			
Lake Shore Inc. (Iron Mt.)				White Pine Copper Corp.			
Lake Superior & Ishpeming RR				Wisc. - MI Power Co.			
Legislature (MI)				WLUC TV - Marquette			
L.H. Shay Veneer				WSOO Radio			
Longyear Realty Co.				WTOM TV Cheboygan			
M.A. Hanna Company				WMUP TV			
Manistique Pulp & Paper Co.							

Figure 15.   *Interorganizational sociometric instrument*

Interaction Structures

To map the dependency patterns among the organizations, we submitted the response choices to a computer matrix rotation process. Each row in the matrix indicated the choices made or given by one respondent for his organization; each column identified the choices received by one organization from all other organizations in the study. Comparing choices given with choices received, we eliminated all non-reciprocated choices from consideration at this point in the analysis.

With the execution of a Boolean matrix, we began by detecting blocks of reciprocally related organizations. The program took each pair of reciprocal choices and searched the matrix for a third organization which was the reciprocal choice of each of the first two. The search was continued for a fourth, fifth, nth organization. The resulting blocks were put on a temporary list until all blocks based on the original pairs of organizations were listed, at which point these blocks were transferred to a permanent list. In this list, any block which was completely included in some other block was eliminated. This produced a list of organizations in which no block was a subset of any other, although members of any one block might be included in other blocks.

The blocks were then arranged on the diagonal with members of the largest block being listed first. The organizations in each succeeding block which were not included in previous blocks were placed in successive rows and columns. This produced matrices of reciprocal choices along the matrix diagonal.

These clusters along the diagonal are referred to as *constellations*. Constellations are a particular configuration of the original blocks chosen so as to display most lucidly the structure of interaction. Constellations, represent specified groupings of organizations, all reciprocally chosen by one another. These are shown in Figure 17 as darkened squares along the diagonal and are labeled A through U. Some reciprocal choices also appear off the diagonal, the number depending upon the complexity of organizational relationships. We believe that of all the possible permutations, this produces a minimum number of off-diagonal configurations.

In order to illustrate the interactions of each organization in relationship to the constellations formed, the idea of constellation sets is introduced. A *constellation set* is a group of organizations, some of which are reciprocally chosen by all members of the constellation called *primary members*; and others which are reciprocally chosen by some, but not all, members of the constellation called *secondary members*.

Organizations that interact with members of more than one constellation set are called liaisons. *Primary liaisons* are primary members of two or more constellation sets; *secondary liaisons* are secondary members of one or more sets and they may be primary members of one (but not more than one) set. Liaisons might be regarded as actual or potential links between constellation sets.

The constellation sets and membership (primary or secondary) of the heterogeneous organizations in the sets are illustrated in Figure 18. The sets are based on reciprocal high frequency interaction linkages among organizations.

Number	Selected Organizations Organization	Scores Received Scores	Rank	Scores Given Scores	Rank
10	City & Village Government	6.46	1	4.25	22
4	Chamber of Commerce	5.87	2	4.94	9
18	Michigan Legislature	5.34	3	3.79	30
12	USDA Forest Service	5.33	4	4.84	12
7	Clairmont Transfer Co.	5.30	5	3.89	29
3	Escaneba Daily Press	5.29	6	7.19	1
14	Soo Line Railroad	5.11	7	4.45	20
17	Cleveland Cliffs Iron Co.	5.04	8	4.45	19
5	UP Power Co.	5.03	9	5.88	4
38	County Road Commissions	4.93	10	3.40	35
2	The Mining Journal	4.91	11	5.52	5
6	Lake Shore Inc.	4.59	12	6.38	3
29	Kimberly Clark of Michigan	4.47	13	3.38	36
24	MSU Cooperative Extension Service	4.46	14	4.48	18
21	Michigan State University	4.43	15	4.10	27
13	Cliffs-Dow Chemical Company	4.32	16	3.75	31
16	Abbott Fox Lumber Company	4.30	17	2.86	45
39	County Sheriffs	4.16	18	2.39	50
45	WLUC-TV	4.11	19	3.46	33
19	County Superintendents of Schools	4.11	20	3.28	39
41	Celotex Corporation	4.03	21	4.20	24
50	City & Village Planning Commissions	4.01	22	2.24	52
20	University of Michigan	4.01	23	4.11	28
49	County Planning Commissions	3.97	24	3.69	32
1	Iron Mountain News	3.96	25	5.42	6
22	UP Tourist Association	3.93	26	6.69	2
36	Milwaukee Road Railroad Company	3.88	27	3.28	40
23	Area Redevelopment Admin. (ARA)	3.63	28	4.14	25
3	Inland Steel Company	3.56	29	4.47	18

	Organization				
8	Wisconsin-Michigan Power Company	3.57	30	4.30	21
46	M.A. Hanna Company	3.55	31	2.61	48
47	Meed Corporation	3.55	32	3.05	42
11	Michigan Economic Expansion Comm.	3.49	33	4.21	23
30	Ahonen Land & Lumber Company	3.37	34	3.45	34
15	Lake Superior & Ishpeming Railroad	3.34	35	4.67	13
55	Michigan Education Association	3.29	36	1.97	60
51	Sawyer-Stoll	3.28	37	2.23	53
37	USDA Soil Conservation Service	3.24	38	4.55	15
33	MI - Wiscon. Timber Products Assoc.	3.22	39	2.02	58
42	General Telephone	3.08	40	3.25	40
54	Connor Land & Lumber Company	3.07	41	2.03	57
48	Pickands-Mather Mining Company	3.05	42	4.65	14
35	White Pine Copper Corporation	3.01	43	3.36	38
53	Republican Party	2.96	44	2.48	49
52	Goodman & Mohawk Lumber Company	2.96	45	2.20	54
40	Democratic Party	2.95	46	5.02	8
26	Keweenaw Land Association, Ltd.	2.91	47	4.88	10
25	FORUM	2.88	48	3.38	37
32	Pettibone Michigan Corporation	2.70	49	4.48	17
27	Longyear Realty Company	2.82	50	4.85	11
28	North Range Mining Company	2.59	51	3.90	28
60	UP Law Enforcement Association	2.57	52	2.07	56
31	Superior Studs, Incorporated	2.57	53	1.98	59
44	Barrett Lumber Company	2.53	54	2.36	51
43	Cloverland REA	2.51	55	2.91	44
34	L.H. Shay Veneer	2.36	56	2.93	43
57	WSOO Radio	2.33	57	5.29	7
58	WMUP-TV	1.99	58	2.61	47
59	Ontonagon Valley REA	1.95	59	2.09	55
56	Drummond Dolomite, Incorporated	1.89	60	1.61	61
61	Teamsters' Union	1.80	61	2.82	45

Figure 16. *Rank ordered organizational sociometric scores received and given by related organizations in Michigan's Upper Peninsula in response to the question, "What organization does your organization deal with in carrying out its business?"*

No.	SELECTED ORGANIZATIONS / ORGANIZATIONS	Grid
1	Iron Mountain News	A
2	The Mining Journal	
3	The Mining Daily Press	B
4	City Chambers of Commerce	C
5	U.P. Power Company	
6	Lake Shore Engineering Inc.	
7	Clairmont Transfer Company	
8	Wisc. - Mich. Power Company	
9	Inland Steel Company	
10	City & Village Government	D
11	Mich. Economic Expansion Comm.	
12	USDA Forest Service	E
13	Cliffs-Dow Chemical	F
14	Soo Line R.R.	G
15	Lake Superior & Ishpeming R.R.	H
16	Abbott Fox Lumber Company	
17	Cleveland Cliffs Iron Company	
18	Michigan Legislature	I
19	County Superintendent of Schools	
20	University of Michigan	J
21	Michigan State University	
22	U.P. Tourist Association	
23	Area Redevelopment Administration	
24	Cooperative Extension Service (MSU)	
25	FORUM	K
26	Keweenaw Land Association Ltd.	L
27	Longyear Reality Company	
28	North Range Mining Company	
29	Kimberly Clark of Michigan	
30	Ahonen Land and Lumber Company	
31	Superior Studs, Inc.	
32	Pettibone Michigan Corp.	
33	Mich. & Wisc. Timber Products Assn.	
34	L.H. Shay Veneer	
35	White Pine Copper Corp.	
36	Milwaukee Road R.R. Company	
37	USDA Soil Conservation Service	
38	County Road Commission	
39	County Sheriff	
40	County Democratic Party	
41	Celotex Corp.	
42	General Telephone	
43	Cleveland REA	
44	Barrett Lumber Company	
45	WLUC-TV Marquette	
46	M.A. Hanna Company	
47	Mead Corp.	
48	Pickands-Mather Mining Company	
49	County Planning Comm.	
50	City & Village Planning Comm.	
51	Sawyer-Stoll	
52	Goodman & Mohawk Lumber Company	
53	County Republican Party	
54	Conner Lumber & Land Company	
55	Michigan Education Association	
56	Drummond Dolomite Inc.	
57	WSOO-Radio	
58	WMUP-TV	
59	Ontonagon Valley REA Power Co.	
60	U.P. Law Enforcement Association	
61	Teamsters' Union	

Organization No.	1	2	3	4	5	6	7	8	9	10	11	12	13	14	15	16	17	18	19	20	21	22	23	24	25	26	27	28

CONSTELLATIONS

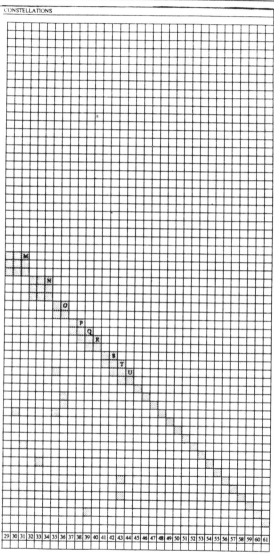

Figure 17.   Matrix representation of constellations formed based on reciprocal choices of 61 organizations in response to question, "What organization does your organization deal with in carrying out its business?"

No.	Selected Organizations	A	B	C	D	E	F	G	H	I	J	K	L	M	N	O	P	Q	R	S	T	U	P	S	Total
																							(Member Frequency)		
1	Iron Mountain News	P.	S	S	S	S	S	S	S	S	S	S	S					S	S				1	7	8
2	The Mining Journal	P.	S	S	S	P.	S	S	S	S	S	S				P.	S		S				2	11	13
3	Escanaba Daily Press	P.	P.	S	P.	S				P.						P.	P.						7	4	11
4	City Chambers of Commerce	P.	P.	P.	S	S	S	S	S	S	S	S											3	5	8
5	UP Power	P.	P.	P.	S	S	S	S	S	S	S	S	S	S	S	S	S			S			3	11	14
6	Lake Shore Engineering Inc	P.	P.	P.	S	S	P.	S	S	S	S	S	S	S	S	S							6	7	13
7	Clairmont Transfer Co.	S	P.	P.			P.	S	S	S										P.	S		2	5	7
8	Wisc. - Mich. Power Co.	S	S	P.				S	S	S			S			S							2	6	8
9	Inland Steel Co.	S	S	P.		S	S	S	S				S										2	6	8
10	City and Village Government	S	S	S	P.	S			S	S	S	S											1	6	7
11	Mich. Economic Expansion Comm.	S	S	S	P.	S					S												1	5	6
12	USDA Forest Service	S	S	S	P.	P.	S	S	S	S	S	S	S			S	S			S			2	11	13
13	Cliffs-Dow Chemical Co.	S	S	S	S	P.	P.	S	S	S					S	S				S		S	2	10	12
14	Soo Line RR	S	S	S	S	S	P.	P.	S			S	S	P.	S	S						S	3	10	13
15	Lake Superior & Ishpeming	S	S	S		S	P.	P.	P.				S	S		S							3	6	9
16	Abbott Fox Lumber Co.	S	S	S		S	P.	P.	P.	P.	S				S	S							2	8	10
17	Cleveland Cliffs Iron Co.	S	S	S	S	S	S	S	P.			S	S						S				1	8	9
18	Michigan Legislature	S	S	S	S				P.	P.	S										S		1	8	9
19	County Superintendent of Schools	S	S			S				P.	P.	S				S	S			S	S		1	6	7
20	University of Michigan	S	S		S	S				P.	P.	P.	S										2	3	5
21	Michigan State University	S	S		S					S	P.	P.	P.				S						1	6	7
22	U.P Tourist Assn.	S	S		S					S	S	P.	P.										1	5	6
23	Area Redevelopment Administration	S				S				S	S	P.	P.										1	4	5
24	Cooperative Extension Service (MSU)	S					S			S	S	P.	P.			S							1	5	6
25	FORUM	S	S			S	S	S	S			P.	S	S						S			1	8	9
26	Keweenaw Land Assn. Ltd.		S	S	S	S						P.	P.										2	5	7
27	Longyear Realty Co.			S	S	S						P.	P.										2	2	4
28	North Range Mining Co.	S		S			S	S	S			S	P.										1	7	8
29	Kimberly Clark of Michigan	S	S	S	S	S	S	S						P.									1	6	7
30	Ahonen Land & Lumber Co.			S	S	S	S							P.									1	4	5
31	Superior Studs, Inc.			S	S		S	S						P.									1	2	3
32	Perthone Mich. Corp.	S	S	S			S	S							P.								1	5	6

33 Mich. & Wisc. Timber Products Assn																					2	3
34 L. H. Shay Veneer																	S	S		1	2	3
35 White Pine Cooper Corp.	S														S	S	S				5	6
36 Milwaukee Road R.R. Co.																S				1	5	6
37 USDA Soil Conservation Service	S								S	S	S				S	S	S	S		1	7	8
38 County Road Commission	S	S							S		S	S			S	S				2	5	7
39 County Sheriff	S	S							S							S			P.	2	3	5
40 County Democratic Party	S							S							S	S			P.	1	4	5
41 Celotex Corp.	S							S								S	S		P.	1	9	10
42 General Telephone				S		S										S		S	S	2	3	5
43 Cloverland REA	S	S		S												S		P.	P.	2	5	7
44 Barrett Lumber Co.			S													S		S	P.	2	3	5
45 WLUC-TV Marquette					S										S	S				6	6
46 M.A. Hanna Co.	S			S	S										S					6	6
47 Mead Corp.	S			S	S	S									S					6	6
48 Pickands-Mather Mining Co.	S														S					7	7
49 County Planning Commission	S					S									S					5	5
50 City & Village Planning Comm.	S			S											S					4	4
51 Sawyer-Stoll							S													3	4
52 Goodman & Mohawk Lumber Co.		S					S								S	S				3	3
53 County Republican Party	S							S							S					3	3
54 Conner Lumber & Land Co.			S				S								S					5	5
55 Michigan Education Association	S											S								2	2
56 Drummond Dolomite Inc.	S		S							S										5	5
57 WSOO-Radio				S	S										S	S				2	2
58 WMUP-TV				S														S		2	3
59 Ontonagon Valley REA Power Co	S																	S		2	3	3
60 U.P. Law Enforcement Assn.																			8	8	3
61 Teamsters' Union	S																		10	10	3
Constellation Frequency	6	5	6	4	5	4	4	4	4	5	3	3	4	3	2	3	3	3	3			
Total	47	44	39	33	24	28	24	25	25	21	21	14	18	19	20	13	14	9	11	13	11	8

Figure 18.   Constellation sets of 61 selected organizations in 21 constellations formed in response to the question, "What organization does your organization deal with in carrying out its business?"

Constellation Sets

The 61 heterogeneous Upper Peninsula organizations included in this study group themselves into 21 identified constellation sets, A through U. The largest set, A, has 47 members and the smallest set, Q, has only seven. The "Constellation Frequency" row at the bottom of Figure 18 indicates the number of organizations holding primary and secondary memberships in each. For example, set A has six primary (organizations 1, 2, 3, 4, 5, 6) and 41 secondary members (organizations 7-26, 28, 29, 32, 35, 37-41, 43, 45-50, 53, 55, 56, 59, 61), for a total membership of 47 organizations. The heterogeneous nature of this constellation set's members can be illustrated by the fact that they represent all 11 economic-interest sectors included in the study.

Constellation Memberships

The Mining Journal (organization 2) is a primary member of constellation sets A and E, and a secondary member of sets B, C, D, F, G, H, I, J, K, P, and R. Some organizations hold memberships in only two constellation sets—e.g., the Michigan Education Association and WSOO Radio (organizations 55 and 57 respectively), while others are members of over 12 of the 21 identified sets—The Mining Journal, U.P. Power Company, Lake Shore Engineering, Inc., USDA Forest Service, Cliffs-Dow Chemical Company, and the Soo Line RR (organizations 2, 5, 6, 12, 13, and 14 respectively). The "Membership Frequency" columns in Figure 18 indicate the number of constellation sets in which each organization holds primary and secondary memberships.

Linkages Between Constellation Sets

The data in Figure 18 indicate that all 21 constellation sets are linked by liaison organizations. Every organization in the study occupies a liaison position. For example, the U.P. Power Company (organization 5) serves as a primary liaison among three sets (A, B, and C) and as a secondary liaison among 11 sets (D, E, F, G, H, J, K, L, O, P, and S). Note how constellation set A is linked to set M through the secondary liaison of Kimberly Clark of Michigan (organization 29), a primary member of set M and a secondary member of set A.

Figures 17 and 18 make it easy to trace many combinations of potential constellation linkages through primary or secondary liaison relationships of members of individual constellation sets. The data illustrate the extensive interrelatedness of organizations as well as of constellation sets. The interaction structure variable is thus clearly identified and represented by the data presented in these figures.

Many explanations could be offered to account for the grouping of organizations in Figures 17 and 18. For example, the first three primary members of coalition set A are daily newspapers owned by a common publisher. The other three primary members, as well as the majority of the secondary members, are organizations whose operations are in large part dependent upon information dissemination, advertising, and promotion.

Three of the primary members of coalition set M represent the manufacturing interest sector. The three organizations are based in different locations in the Upper Peninsula and are tied together by the common ownership of one of the organizations by the other two.

The interdependence of the primary members of coalition sets B, C, and D is not based on either common ownership or common functions. These organizations are reputational leaders among organizations comprising communications, tourism, utilities, manufacturing, transportation, mining, forestry, and government services, composing eight of the 11 economic-interest sectors studied (as indicated by the original nominations). This interdependent grouping of influential organizations from different interest sectors can be theoretically accounted for, but without the aid of the sociometric measurement probably could not have been easily identified. The sociometric technique, then, provides a convenient mechanism for ordering and mapping the relationships of formally unstructured interaction patterns among heterogeneous organizations.

Influence Patterns

Our analysis of the "influence patterns" variable was made in terms of values assigned for reciprocal relationships and are shown in Figure 19. This analysis rests on the assumption that high frequency business ratings serve as indicators of high levels of influence. In the procedures used, a value of 1 is given for each reciprocal bond an organization has with each primary member of each constellation set.

Iron Mountain News (organization 1) has reciprocal bonds with all five primary member organizations of set A; therefore, it is assigned a membership value of **5** in cell A of the matrix in Figure 19. The News has four reciprocal bonds with primary member organizations of set B, so the value assigned in matrix cell B is **4**, as is the case with set C. Since Iron Mountain News has reciprocal bonds with only one primary member of constellation sets D, M, and R, values of **1** are assigned in the corresponding matrix cells. A value of **2** is assigned for its bonds with set J. Because no bonds are established for sets E, F, G, H, I, K, L, N, O, P, Q, S, T, and U, no values are assigned in these cells.

The constellation membership values (Figure 19) of Iron Mountain News indicate that the organization is a highly influential member of sets A, B, and C, and a less influential member of sets D, J, M, and I. The Teamsters' Union (organization 61) on the other hand, with values of 1, 2, 1 for sets A, B, and C, respectively, and no values assigned for sets D through U, is not a highly influential member of any of the 21 constellation sets in the study.

Status Arrangements

The *status arrangement* variable may be analyzed in terms of scored measures. These measures consist of a score for each organization, called a *membership score*, and a score for each constellation set, called a *constellation set score*. The scores are derived from the constellation set membership value matrix shown in Figure 19. A total membership value for a given organization is obtained by summing across the row for the organization in question; the organization's membership score is then computed by expressing the organization's total membership value as a percentage of the sum of all total membership values obtained from the sample, multiplied by 100. For Iron Mountain News, the score calculated is 2.51. This procedure is repeated for all organizations in the matrix.

Analogously, constellation set scores, shown in Figure 19, are obtained by first summing each column for a given constellation set to obtain total constellation set values, and then converting these total constellation set values into constellation set scores by expressing them as percentages of the sum of all total constellation set values and multiplying by 100. In the case of constellation set A, the score calculated is 16.02. As a result of this computational process, both the column of membership scores and the row of constellation scores will sum to 100.

This analysis rests on the assumption that such a scoring system serves as an indicator of status. The data presented in Figure 19 show that the Escanaba Daily Press (organization 3), Lake Shore Engineering, Inc. (6), Upper Peninsula Power Company (5), and The Mining Journal (2) exhibit the greatest amount of high-level reciprocal interaction, with respective membership scores of 4.32, 4.18, 4.04, and 4.02. These data are interpreted to mean that organizations 3, 6, 5, and 2 are highly influential and deeply involved in the interorganizational economic business activities of the Upper Peninsula; on this basis they are also identified as high status Upper Peninsula organizations.

The data in Figure 19 show that constellation sets A, B, and C exhibit the greatest amount of high-level reciprocal interaction among their member organizations, as indicated by respective constellation set scores of 16.02, 13.51, and 12.95. This indicates high-level interorganizational interaction in Upper Peninsula affairs among constellation sets as well as among their organization members. Therefore, these three constellation sets are considered to be the most influential, high-status sets affecting economic business activities in Michigan's U.P. at the time of the study. Status arrangements of individual organizations as well as of constellation sets are thus reflected in the rank-order designations ascribed to each organization and constellation set in Figure 19.

Many explanations could be offered to account for the grouping of organizations in Figures 17, 18, and 19. Constellation set formation can be accounted for on the basis of factors such as —

* **Complementary differences**—heterogeneous, autonomous organizations from widely diverse interest sectors and wide geographic bases of operation group together.

* **Supplementary similarity**—homogeneous, autonomous organizations from common interest sectors, with or without a common geographic area, group together.

* **Common ownership.**

* **A common geographic basis of operation.**

The point is that once the constellation sets are identified, explanations for such formations are in order and can be made for each set represented in the matrix.

No	Selected Organizations	A	B	C	D	E	F	G	H	I	J	K	L	M	N	O	P	Q	R	S	T	U	Member Scores	Rank Order
1	Iron Mountain News	3	4	4		2					2	1	1						1				2.51	15
2	The Mining Journal	3	4	3	2	2	2	1	2		4	1		1			1		1				4.02	3
3	Escanaba Daily Press	3	4	4	3	1	1				4	1					2	2	2				4.32	1
4	City Chambers of Commerce	3	4	3	1	1	1			1													2.65	8
5	U.P. Power Company	5	4	3	2	1	2	1			1	2	1			1	1	1		1		1	4.04	4
6	Lake Shore Engineering Co.	5	4	3	2	1		1			1				1	1	1				1	1	4.18	2
7	Charmont Transfer Company	4	4	5				1	2														2.51	12
8	Wisc.-Michigan Power Company	4	4	5				1	1					1						2		1	2.65	10
9	Inland Steel Company	3	4	5		1	1	1	2			1	1			1							2.51	13
10	City & Village Government	5	3	2	3	1				2	2												2.51	14
11	Mich. Economic Expansion Comm	2	2	1	3					4	4												1.81	20
12	USDA Forest Service	2	1		3	2	2	1	1		1	2	2	2			1					1	2.79	7
13	Cliffs-Dow Chemical Company	4	3	3	1	2	3	2	1		1	1								1		1	3.2	5
14	Soo Line RR	2	2	2	1	1	3	3	2				1	3	1	1							3.06	6
15	Lake Superior Ispeming RR	1	2	3		2	3	3	3				1		1								2.23	17
16	Abbott Fox Lumber Co.	1	2	3	1		3	2	3		1	1			1								2.65	9
17	Cleveland Cliffs Iron Company	3	3	4			1	2	3			1	1							2			2.65	11
18	Michigan Legislature	2	2	1	1					3	1						1	1	1				1.81	21
19	County Superintendent of Schools	1	1							3	1							1		1	1		1.25	34
20	University of Michigan	2	1		1					3	4						1						1.53	28
21	Michigan State University	3	2	1	1				1	1	4												1.81	22
22	U.P. Tourist Association	5	3	2	2					1	4												2.37	16
23	Area Redevelopment Administration	1								1	4												1.25	35
24	Cooperative Extension Service (MSU)	1		2	1	1			1														1.39	30
25	FORUM	3	2	1		1	1					2	2										1.95	19
26	Keweenaw Land Association Ltd.	1	1	1	1	1						2	3										1.39	31
27	Longyear Realty Company	1		1	1							2	3										0.97	44
28	North Range Mining Company	1	1	2			2	2	2			2	3										2.09	18

Constellation Set Membership Value

#	Organization	A	B	C	D	E	F	G	H	I	J	K	L	M	N	O	P	Q	R	S	T	U	Score	Idx
29	Kimberly Clark of Michigan	1		2	1	1	1	1	1														1.25	36
30	Ahonen Land & Lumber Company	1		2	1	1	1	1	1														0.97	45
31	Superior Studs, Inc					1	1	1	1														0.7	49
32	Pettibone Michigan Corp.	1		2	2		1	1	1						2								1.25	37
33	Mich. & Wisc. Timber Products Assn.					1	1	1	1						2								0.56	53
34	L. H. Shay Veneer								1						2					1			0.56	54
35	White Pine Copper Corp.	2		3	3			1	2							1							1.53	26
36	Milwaukee Road R.R. Company			1	1		1	2	2							1	1						1.25	38
37	USDA, Soil Conservation Service	2			1	1					1	2						1					1.53	27
38	County Road Commission	2		2							1							2	2			1	1.53	25
39	County Sheriff	2		1															2	2			0.97	42
40	County Democratic Party	1		1														1		2			1.11	40
41	Celotex Corp.	1		1	2	1	1	2	1		1	1							1		2	1	1.81	23
42	General Telephone	1		1	1																2		0.7	48
43	Cloverland REA	1		1	1	1	2	2	1		1				1						1		0.97	43
44	Barrett Lumber Company			2	1	1	2	1	1			3											1.11	39
45	WLUC-TV Marquette	2		2	2	1	1															1	1.53	29
46	M.A. Hanna Company	2		3	4			1	1				1			1							1.67	24
47	Mead Corp.	2		3	2			1	1							1	1						1.39	32
48	Pickands-Mather Mining Company	1		1	2		1					2	2			1	1						1.39	33
49	County Planning Commission	2		2	1																		1.11	41
50	City & Village Planning Commission	2		2	1			2			2	2	1										0.84	46
51	Sawyer-Stoll						1	1	2	1													0.84	47
52	Goodman & Mohawk Lumber Company	3						1	1					1							1		0.56	55
53	County Republican Party			1		1	1																0.7	50
54	Conner Lumber & Land Company					1					2					1							0.7	51
55	Michigan Education Association	1		1	1				1														0.42	38
56	Drummond Dolomite Inc.	1		1															1				0.7	52
57	WSOO-Radio				1	1																	0.28	61
58	WMUP-TV				1																		0.42	59
59	Ontonagon Valley REA Power Co	1		1	2	1	1											1			1		0.56	56
60	U.P. Law Enforcement Association	1			1																		0.42	60
61	Teamsters' Union	1		2	1																		0.56	57
	Constellation Set	A	B	C	D	E	F	G	H	I	J	K	L	M	N	O	P	Q	R	S	T	U		
	Constellation Set Score	16.	13.5	13.	5.57	3.9	5.85	5.01	4.4	4.04	6.96	2.79	3.2	2.51	1.67	1.81	1.95	1.53	1.53	1.81	1.39	1.53	100	
	Rank Order	1	2	3	6	10	5	7	8	9	4	12	11	13	17	15	14	18	19	16	21	20		

Figure 19. Constellation sets and membership scores of 61 selected organizations in 21 constellations formed in response to the question, "What organization does your organization deal with in carrying out its business?"

Some formations could have been predicted on the basis of existing sociological organizational classification schemes; many, however, would have been missed. If, after testing for validation, this tendency persists when this technique is used, then we will have added to sociological understanding of interorganizational relationships.

Analysis by Homogeneous Groupings

The data obtained from the sociometric technique also lend themselves to more traditional organizational analysis. The organizations can be classified as public or private, profit or nonprofit, or any other grouping of sociological interest. To illustrate this, we have rearranged the matrix, classifying the organizations by the primary interest or interest sector of each organization (Figure 20). For the 11 specified interest sectors (mining, forestry, service, etc.), sociometric scores were obtained of the perceived business interaction among the organizations composing them.

Because organizations do not have a frequency of interaction score for interaction with themselves, zeros appear along the principal diagonal of the matrix, as specified above, making the determination of an interest sector's average frequency of interaction between organizations in that interest sector a special case which must allow for the theoretically "empty cells" along the diagonal. Consequently, the average frequency of interaction score for organizations in the first interest sector with organizations in the first interest sector is given.

INTEREST SECTORS	Transportation	Education	Services	Tourism	Manufacturing	Forestry	Mining	Communications	Utilities	Agriculture	Fishing	TOTAL GIVEN
Tourism	8.38	8.44	7.85	9.00	5.80	4.25	5.83	8.17	5.17	3.75	4.0	6.69
Communications	4.30	5.96	5.38	5.69	2.64	3.09	3.07	3.48	4.19	3.13	2.13	4.00
Transportation	5.34	3.02	3.79	3.30	5.65	2.83	5.45	2.63	3.20	2.10	1.60	3.93
Education	3.69	7.60	4.85	6.25	2.69	2.79	2.74	4.01	2.33	4.13	3.33	3.91
Utilities	5.13	3.81	3.86	4.13	3.40	3.78	3.77	3.67	5.10	1.75	2.50	3.79
Mining	6.05	3.78	3.71	2.29	2.90	3.07	5.10	2.86	3.14	1.11	2.14	3.58
Forestry	3.82	3.10	2.91	3.29	5.31	5.45	3.80	2.29	2.36	1.50	1.00	3.48
Manufacturing	5.51	3.44	3.03	2.00	4.56	4.60	3.15	2.40	2.58	1.13	1.25	3.40
Services	3.74	4.77	4.62	3.68	2.00	2.17	1.88	4.01	2.21	2.61	3.00	3.25
Fishing	4.13	3.56	2.15	2.50	1.80	2.13	2.25	3.17	3.83	1.75	1.00	2.61
Agriculture	1.81	4.17	2.63	1.38	1.68	1.97	1.48	2.81	2.21	3.75	1.75	2.37
TOTAL RECEIVED	4.50	4.44	3.97	3.55	3.37	3.31	3.23	3.23	2.91	2.24	2.13	3.55

Possible Score Range - 1.00 - 9.00   Rows = Scores Given
Columns = Scores Received   High Interacting Interest Sectors = Scores ≥ 4.00

Figure 20.   Sociometric scores given and received by specified interest sectors in Michigan's Upper Peninsula in response to the question, "What organization does your organization deal with in carrying out its business?"

Two sets of scores were obtained, one denoting the sociometric score received by an interest sector from all others, and one containing the sociometric score given by each sector to all other interest sectors (see Figure 20). It was arbitrarily decided that scores received or given above the 4.00 level would be considered indicative of "high" inter-action. Like the scores of individual organizations, these scores may serve as indicators of the relative amounts of interaction, influence, and status of interest-sector groupings of organizations.

In Figure 20, sociometric scores given and received within and across 11 specified interest sectors are presented in rank order. The interaction of one interest sector with all others is shown in the "Total Given" column and "Total Received" row of Figure 20. The tourism sector ranks first in scores given, with a sociometric score of 6.69, followed by communication (4.00), transportation (3.93), education (3.91), utilities (3.79), mining (3.58), forestry (3.48), manufacturing (3.40), services (3.25), fishing (2.61), and agriculture (2.37). With the exception of the tourism and communications interest sectors' high interaction with other sectors studied, these data indicate a relatively low interaction pattern between any given interest sector and all other interest sectors in the study. This same pattern holds for scores received, with transportation ranking first and receiving a sociometric score of 4.50 from all other interest sectors, followed by education (4.44), services (3.97), tourism (3.55), manufacturing (3.37), forestry (3.31), mining (3.23), communications (3.23), utilities (2.91), agriculture

(2.24), and fishing (2.13) sectors. These findings are not surprising when consideration is given to the averaging effect of such an analysis.

Quite a different pattern emerges when the scores of pairs of interest sectors are examined. Note, for example, that the transportation sector receives high sociometric scores from the tourism (8.38), communications (4.30), utilities (5.13), mining (6.05), manufacturing (5.51), and fishing (4.13) interest sectors. At the same time, the transportation sector gives reciprocal high interaction scores only to the manufacturing (5.65) and mining (5.45) sectors. These data clearly indicate that six of the ten interest sectors perceive their businesses as being dependent upon high frequency dealing with transportation sector organizations. However, this perceived high-level interaction dependency is not reciprocated by the transportation sector except in relation to the manufacturing and mining sectors. This nonreciprocated relationship may well be interpreted to be a normal, desirable interaction arrangement among these interest-sector organizations.

It is also interesting to note the low-level interaction patterns existing between transportation and agriculture (2.10 and 1.81), education and transportation (3.69 and 3.02), services and fishing (3.00 and 2.15), manufacturing and agriculture (1.13 and 1.68), forestry and agriculture (1.50 and 1.97), mining and agriculture (1.11 and 1.48), communications and forestry (3.09 and 2.29), and utilities and agriculture (1.75 and 2.21). These data indicate the highly discriminating way that interest sector organizations tend to interact with one another.

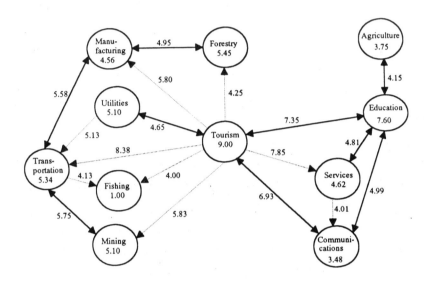

Figure 21.   *Sociogram reflecting perceived high interaction among interest sectors in Michigan's Upper Peninsula in response to the question, "What organization does your organization deal with in carrying out its business?"*

Organizations within a given interest sector also exhibit varying interaction patterns. For example, units making up the transportation sector give and receive from each other a sociometric value of 5.34. This indicates that a relatively high frequency of business-dealing interaction occurs among the organizations within the transportation sector. High-level interaction within interest sectors is also indicated in the education (7.60), services (4.62), tourism (9.00), manufacturing (4.56), forestry (5.45), mining (5.10), and utilities (5.10) sectors. On the other hand, low frequency interaction patterns are evident in the communications (3.48), agriculture (3.75), fishing (1.00) interest sectors. These scores indicate a pattern of high-level interorganizational dependencies among organizations in sectors such as education, and competitive or low-level interaction dependency patterns among organizations in the communications, agriculture, and fishing interest sectors.

In general, the data in Figure 21 indicate a great deal of selective variation in the interaction patterns both within and across interest sectors. The data provide a basis for ascribing interaction and influence as well as status interpretations to the analysis.

The sociogram presented in Figure 21 reflects the perceived high-level (sociometric score ≥ 4.00) business interaction within and among the interest sectors in Michigan's Upper Peninsula. Each sociometric bond reflects what can be called a perceived high business interaction relationship. Reciprocal relationships are represented by solid lines. The arrows attached to each indicate the direction (score given or score received) of the relationship. In Figure 21, the two scores were averaged and presented as one score representing scores given and scores received. One way nonreciprocated scores given are represented is by a dotted line with the arrow designating the direction of the bond. Sociometric scores reported on each line represent a measure of frequency of interaction between the sectors connected by that line. Scores presented in each circle represent interaction frequency among the organizations comprising that specific interest sector. We interpret these data to mean that the higher the sociometric score, the higher the intensity or strength of the bond.

This picture of interaction among interest sectors distinguishes three rather interesting groupings. For the criterion of general business interaction, it appears that the service, communications, and education sectors form one constellation set, and that the tourism, communications, and education sectors form another. The intensity or strength of the interaction bonds among the four interest sectors making up these two constellation sets ranges from a sociometric score of 4.01, given by service to communications and by communications to education, to a score of 8.44, given by tourism to education, (Figures 20 and 21).

A different, chain-type formation is made up of the mining, transportation, manufacturing, and forestry sectors (Figures 20 and 21). In this grouping the transportation and manufacturing sectors occupy positions of *relative centrality*. The transportation sector occupies a central, but not reciprocal, position with four other interest sectors — communication, fishing, utilities, and tourism. The intensity of the bonds among the four interest sectors making up this chain-type formation ranges from a sociometric score of 4.60, given by manufacturing to forestry, to 5.65, given by transportation to manufacturing.

Agriculture is reciprocally linked only to the education sector, with scores of 4.17 and 4.13 or 4.15 average. The fishing sector has no reciprocal attachments and thereby lies on the periphery of interaction activity among the groupings formed from the data obtained in this study.

The overall pattern emerging from this analysis calls attention to the fact that the tourism sector appears to provide a linking function between public service and product-oriented interest sectors (Likert, 1961). This is true when consideration is given to the fact that organizations comprising the tourism, service, education, and communications interest sectors are oriented to public service, while the organizations comprising the agriculture, fishing, mining, transportation, utilities, manufacturing, and forestry interest sectors have product/ production or profit-making orientations.

Conclusions

Our application of sociometric techniques to the study of organizations was an attempt to answer the question, "Can sociometry be transposed to the organizational level?" Our answer is, "Yes!"

In adapting the sociometric technique for use with organizations, we used the computer to trace the sociometric linkages that emerged. The use of our computer matrix rotation process extended the size of the universe that could be analyzed by sociometric techniques. With our program, a matrix of over 200 respondents can be dealt with in a very concise and clear manner; now computer capacity rather than human capacity is the limiting factor to the size of a manageable sociometric universe.

In our application of sociometric methods to organizational interaction, we confronted some problems peculiar to the new subject matter. The first of these was that respondents had to report not on their own personal interaction with other persons, but on the interaction of their organization with 60 other designated organizations. Primarily because of resource limitations for the Upper Peninsula case study, we decided to use only one respondent from each organization. This no doubt increased the chance for respondent errors. Research is needed on the reliability of informants used in this way. For this study, we assumed that the informants, being high-ranking officials empowered to speak for their respective organizations, were well informed and could reliably reflect their organization's business relations with other organizations.

Regardless of the problems raised by the use of one informant for each organization, we did obtain information of the same kind as could be obtained from interviewing a number of informants and pooling their answers. The techniques of sociometric analysis would be the same regardless of the kind and number of informants used to represent each organizational unit.

Another methodological problem was determining how many and what kind of questions to ask about relations between organizations. In this report we have illustrated how the responses to one question, "What organization does your organization deal with (frequently, occasionally, never) in carrying out its business?" were analyzed. In our larger research project, five questions, each designed to measure different types of interdependence, were used, and slightly different patterns of interaction emerged from each question. In our study we theorized that business relations are of central importance in economic development affairs and that the structure revealed by the responses to the above question would be meaningful. Regardless of the theory and the content of the questions, however, the same procedures of sociometric analysis can be applied.

Using the sociometric technique, we confirmed our hunch that organizations vary and are highly selective in their degree of interdependence with others in the field. The interpretation we gave to the data is that organizations which are primary members of the larger constellation sets and which have reciprocal relations with the largest number of other organizations are the most influential with respect to the economic development of the region.

As expected, a substantial proportion of the organizations can be grouped into a few constellation sets on the basis of reciprocal sociometric choices. The first three sets include 49 of the organizations. The 10 largest sets delineated include all 61 of the organizations, 25 of them as primary members and the remainder as secondary members. These constellation sets are not isolated from one another, but are linked by common members. Every organization was found to be linked to every other organization through its constellation set.

After identifying organizational dependencies, we found that they could be accounted for and explained on the basis of—

*   **Complementary differences,** in which influential hetero-
       geneous, autonomous organizations from widely different
       interest sectors and wide geographic bases of operation
       grouped together.

*   **Supplementary similarity,** in which homogeneous, autono-
       mous organizations from common interest sectors, with or
       without a common geographic area, group together.

*   **Common ownership.**

*   **A common geographic basis of operation.**

The significance of this fact is that once the coalition sets are
identified, explanations for such formations can be made for each set in
the matrix.

Some of the formations which emerged could have been predicted
on the basis of existing sociological organizational classification
schemes; many, however, would have been missed. For example, identification of organizations comprising interaction sets B and C would be
difficult if not impossible without the aid of sociometric techniques. Yet
understanding the dependency patterns of those heterogeneous,
geographically dispersed organizations is important for explaining why
and how economic development occurs in the Upper Peninsula.

In this study we highlighted which interorganizational structures
emerge simply on the basis of matching high frequency reciprocal
sociometric choices. Once the sociometric data are obtained, we also
illustrated the possibility of carrying out a number of other analytic
procedures. For example, we computed the total sociometric scores

received by each organization and rank-ordered the organizations according to amount of dependency. We also analyzed scores given and received by organizations using interest-sector groupings as a control variable. The data also lend themselves to more traditional organizational analysis; the organizations can be classified by interest sectors, as public or private, profit or nonprofit, or by any other grouping of sociological interest. Interorganizational sociometric data may also be subjected to more sophisticated analytical techniques such as Lingoes' Smallest Space Analyses (1966; Levine 1972). The sociometric technique, then, can provide the data for many different kinds of analyses of inter-organizational relationships.

Chapter 11

AN INTERORGANIZATIONAL APPROACH TO THE EXPLANATION OF COMMUNITY DEVELOPMENT ACTIVITIES[1]

Knowledge is acquired through research, through synthesis, through practice, and teaching. These four categories—the scholarship of discovery, of integration, of application and teaching—are tied inseparably to each other (Boyer 1990).

The study of organizations involved in community development activities is a generally neglected field. This is true despite the fact that community development is, first and foremost, an interorganizational phenomenon. Few, if any, development projects can be initiated and completed by a single community, organization, and certainly not by an individual. True, an individual might conceive the idea, may even propose the suggested development to the community. But very early in the process, various groups, organizations, or agencies become involved.

---

[1]This work first appeared in *Clinical Sociology Review* Vol. 4, 1986, and is printed here with the Journal's permission.

Social institutions must, in general, become involved to allocate the necessary resources; employ, persuade, and assign the personnel needed to do the work; review the plans; and grant the permits to proceed. In fact, most development projects require the involvement and cooperation of many organizations, as well as cooperative action on the part of many individuals.

Despite this recognition of the interdependency of organizations, it is rare to find research that penetrates this interorganizational phenomenon. My objective in this chapter is to develop a theory for use in the study of the interorganizational relationships of society within a community development context.

Community development is best conceptualized as planned change. Contrary to the general notion that communities—and specifically organizations—tend to resist change, my research and programming experience over the past 35 years suggest just the opposite; they welcome change. Planned change, i.e., community development, in fact, is sought by individuals, small groups, and organizations alike—but with certain conditions. As exchange theorists have pointed out, there are significant human and material costs associated with change. If development is to occur, the costs must be perceived by the participants to be less than the probable gain. Planned change must pass the test of acceptability and validation by the participating units.

No innovations or new practices will be adopted until each development goal has met the validation test of each affected group. If the groups that will be significantly affected do not approve the proposed change, they may mobilize to resist it. This resistance is not so much an inherent opposition to change as it is a failure of the proposed development to meet the validation tests that must be passed before adoption and implementation occur. While there is little or no systematic data on how this process takes place, interorganizational research does provide clues that are useful in theorizing about various dimensions of organization involvement in community development activities. The following generalizations flow from such studies (Anderson 1963, 1964, 1976; Anderson and Gendell 1981; Long et al. 1973; March and Simon 1959; Miller 1952; Sower et al. 1957):

* Modern society is bureaucratic. Its functional requirements are generally the responsibility of organizations.

* Organizations are the basic units of social power.

* As such, they are responsible for development. Societal development is carried out by some combination of large, small, simple, complex, public, or private organizations.

* Organizations are units of various subsystems of society at large. These organizations are created, controlled, and operated in an interorganizational environment, and each organization's survival is dependent upon this environment. The growth and/or decline of a society is a function of the interrelationships among the organizations of that society.

* Organizations are control mechanisms through which power for development is generated and flows. They represent basic units which receive, hold and allocate resources. Consequently, organizations, in themselves, can be viewed as a basic resource of development activity.

* Social power is structured and the social structure of a community or a region is made up of interdependent, heterogeneous, interacting organizations.

*   The organizations within a community or region can be
     seen as having a set of roles that constitute the social
     organization of that region. Within this structure, individual
     organizations typically act and contribute in accordance
     with role prescriptions or expectations. They perform and
     coordinate their activities with one another in accordance
     with the relationship of their own roles to the roles of
     others in the structure.

*   Organizations form constellations in order to achieve
     development goals. As specific issues arise, overlapping
     constellations of special interest organizations are formed.
     A specific organization sometimes cooperates, at other
     times competes, and at still other times is not involved with
     other organizations in issue resolution. (Anderson 1976,
     and Chapter 10).

*   A given organization's involvement and influence in the
     resolution of an issue or specific development project
     depend upon the place it occupies in the order of the
     organized constellation of organizations affected by the
     issue or the developmental activity. For any given issue,
     some organizations are more powerful than others. An
     organization's power rank will generally vary with the
     nature of the issue to be resolved.

In addition, classical diffusion studies provide additional under-
pinning for the generation of a theory of development at the community
level (Rogers 1975, 1983; Rogers and Agarwala-Rogers 1976; Rogers
et al.   1969; Utterback 1974). While most diffusion research has
focused on how innovation decisions are made, by whom, using what
criteria, and with what consequences within a single organization, these
studies only hint at variations in adoption practices at the interorganizational level. Diffusion researchers generally assume that it is rational
(good) to adopt innovations and that the rejection of an innovation is an

undesirable (bad) and/or irrational decision. However, a few of these researchers have pointed out that this value aspect of diffusion and adoption literature is more a rationale than a fact. What is needed is the development of some criteria by which the judgment to adopt or not adopt is explained.

An Interorganizational Explanation of Community Development Activities

Here I present an interorganizational theory that accounts for and explains the adoption and implementation of innovative ideas at the community level. This theory is a result of my research and practical experiences along with those of other researchers and applied development specialists working in Community Development Programs at Michigan State University (Anderson 1963, 1964, 1976; Anderson and Gendell 1981; Long et al. 1973; Sower et al. 1957).

The theory attempts to account for how organizational responses to an innovative idea occur. It provides for a flow chart on the adoption of an innovative idea in a community and identifies a relevant order of organizations whose unilateral responses to the innovation determine whether the idea is adopted and implemented. Conditions that contribute to interorganizational coupling of organizational innovations are discussed. The theory identifies organizational conditions favorable for adoption. It predicts organizational members' response to the implementation of innovative ideas based on the kind of power used.

The primary variables in the theory are organizational involvement and adoption and implementation of innovations at the community level. These variables are related to organization type and power used. Other

variables, such as structure, administrative style, membership characteristics, prestige, and organizational dependence, also affect organizational
involvement, but are dealt with only indirectly.

The nature and timing of organizational involvement and adoption
or rejection of community development proposals are the bases for
classification and analysis. Organizational involvement and adoption
processes are related as well to other development variables. Furthermore, organizations with different adoption processes tend to differ in
the way they react to community development activities over time.
Organizations serve as the collectives within which the general problem
of community development may be studied empirically. They constitute
a "strategic site" (Morton 1959) for the study of community development activities because community development is dependent upon the
interaction in and among organizations.

Interorganizational Action Is Required for Collective Community Decisions

The adoption and implementation of an innovative idea in a
community requires that several organizations in a community come
together and group their ideas, personnel, and resources to implement
an innovation in the community. These organizations must come from
the relevant order, which is all organizations that perceive themselves or
are perceived as having the socially defined right to pass judgment on
the "idea" because they may be directly affected by its implementation.

Clues as to how implementation takes place are provided by
Loumann and Pappi (1976) in their study of how collective decisions
were taken in several cities in Germany. They found that the principle of

sector differentiation—that is, determining the interorganizational relationships of the relevant order of community organizations—is more important in structuring group space than is the relative positioning of individual community elites in their personal networks.

Loumann and Pappi conducted a network analysis in which they identified sets of principal organizations, the social structures, and the underlying processes of the organization decision-making network. It was, in effect, a study of the differentiation and integration of large-scale, complex social systems. Using Parsons' (1960) paradigm of money, power, influence, and commitment as the integrative mechanisms of complex society, they viewed an organization as an input-output system in which transactions between systems are consequential in the internal maintenance of the system as well as in changing the internal components. Structural differentiation of social systems over time leads to subsystems in which organizations take on functionally more specialized roles that are essential to the operation of the larger system. The interchange between these subsystem organizations serves to regulate the levels of activities among and between them. This specialization results in a higher level of selective dependency among organizations in a community setting.

According to Loumann and Pappi, "large-scale systems are usually differentiated around at least two axes or dimensions":

The Adaptive Axis: The extent and character of the division of labor of the system—i.e., differentiation—resulting in a number of population groups differing significantly from each other in work activities, and in rewards and privileges associated with these activities.

For this work, differentiation of relevant order organizations occurs based on claims for scarce goods, service facilities, etc. Differentiation is based on each organization's unique contribution necessary to the adoption of an innovative idea at the community level.

The Pattern-Maintenance Axis: The differentiation of the population into subgroups holding distinctive social values regarding the desirable or ideal state of the system. For this work, differentiation based on evaluative standards depends on values used in setting priorities among organizational goals by each organization in the relevant order.

The following postulates represent reformulations of Loumann and Pappi's work:

Postulate I
Relationship-Specific Structures: In any community there exist a multiplicity of social structures that give rise to many types of social relationships linking one structure to another.

Postulate II
Distance-Generating Mechanisms: For any given relationship-specific structure, there exists a principle of systematic bias in channeling the formation of, or in making more likely, the relationship between certain kinds of structures and the avoidance of such relationships among others.

Postulate III
Structural Contradictions: Given the many relationship-specific structures predicated on different principles of organization, structural contradictions are likely features of any community.

Loumann and Pappi's work, as does Etzioni's (1975) and mine, suggests at least three concepts of integration of community organizations that account for how the interorganizational phenomenon of community decision making occurs. They are summarized as follows:

The administrative concept of integration is based on the grounds of "functional necessity." Some specialized subset of actors representing the relevant order in the system assumes responsibility for managing the diverse, functionally differentiated activities of its components, in order to achieve system goals. This is a highly intense, centralized, and, when necessary, forceful implementation of the integrative process. It may be viewed as an impersonal, ordered, compliance concept.

The utilitarian tradition concept of integration is based on an economic model in which functions serve as an integrative or collective decision-making mechanism. An example is the competitive interaction of organizations in the market place; their producing, buying, and selling bring about an equilibrium between levels of production and consumption. This tends to be an impersonal, economic, market force concept.

The social choice concept of integration assumes higher moral values on the part of component actors and organizations in an effort to influence collective decisions. It is a system in which component actors and organizations have greater or lesser impact in determining the outcomes of particular collective decisions based on the dominant values employed. It assumes the willingness of some component actors and organizations to act in concert to influence the decision outcome. This is an impersonal—this time represented as a basic cultural—bargaining, or political action concept.

The Adoption of an Innovative Idea at the Community Level

Organizational behavior that is supported by a society or by a community is not easily changed. In a very real sense, this represents a

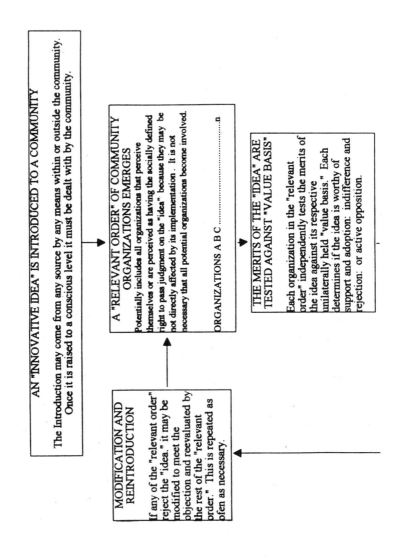

AN "INNOVATIVE IDEA" IS INTRODUCED TO A COMMUNITY

The introduction may come from any source by any means within or outside the community. Once it is raised to a conscious level it must be dealt with by the community.

A "RELEVANT ORDER" OF COMMUNITY ORGANIZATIONS EMERGES

Potentially includes all organizations that perceive themselves or are perceived as having the socially defined right to pass judgment on the "idea" because they may be not directly affected by its implementation. It is not necessary that all potential organizations become involved.

ORGANIZATIONS A B C ....n

THE MERITS OF THE "IDEA" ARE TESTED AGAINST "VALUE BASIS"

Each organization in the "relevant order" independently tests the merits of the idea against its respective unilaterally held "value basis." Each determines if the idea is worthy of support and adoption: indifference and rejection: or active opposition.

MODIFICATION AND REINTRODUCTION

If any of the "relevant order" reject the "idea," it may be modified to meet the objection and reevaluated by the rest of the "relevant order." This is repeated as often as necessary.

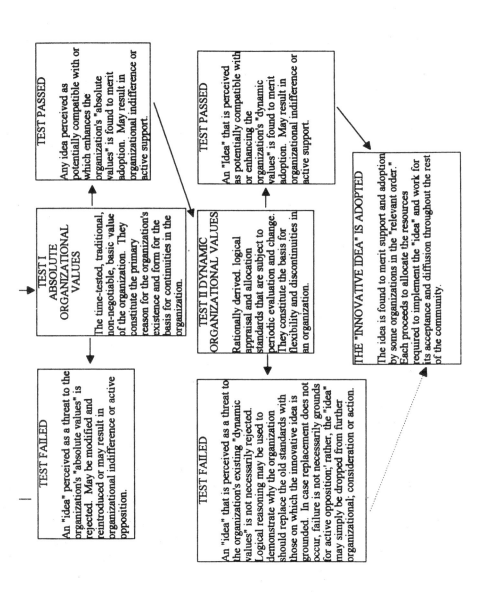

Figure 22.   *A model for the adoption of an innovative idea in a community*

condition of "if it's not broken, don't fix it." Organizations in such a position are unlikely to sense a need for change, least of all innovative change. If such change threatens the possible loss of social support, the organization will avoid it. In addition, organizational change is resisted when it is perceived as an imposition of values foreign to the community and culture (Burns and Stalker 1961; Kanter 1983).

According to Kelman and Warwick (1973), adoption of new patterns requires unfreezing existing patterns and overcoming resistance either by challenging or undermining social support for existing patterns, or by minimizing or removing the perceived threat such a change poses for the existing support patterns. Organizations expose themselves to communications about new ideas only to the extent that change is perceived as relevant to the achievement of their more important goals and purposes. But organizations active in a social environment cannot entirely avoid exposure to societal communications and ideas, new or old, supportive of or critical to the organization's place in its environment. Ideas abound, and organizations are bombarded from within by members, from without by individuals and organizations who are dependent users of the organization's products, by both enemies and friendly cohorts, and by individuals and other organizations that are not even aware of the organization's existence.

When innovative ideas are called to the organization's attention, they must be dealt with. Figure 22 provides a general model of how innovative ideas are dealt with by organizations within a community.

Coupling of Interests

The adoption of an innovative idea at the community level is not only an organizational phenomenon, it is interorganizational in character. A sufficient number of organizations from the relevant order unilaterally may find the idea meritorious of adoption; however, no one organization alone can implement the idea, however worthy it is. Implementation requires the coupling, the coming together and sharing resources, by a number of independent organizations with distinctly different values, purposes, structures, and resource bases (see the development organization concept in Chapter 8).

These different kinds of organizations, in effect, represent centers of knowledge specialization necessary to implement the idea. The coupling process is similar in its operation to the coupling of knowledge that Morton (1971) describes in his study of innovation within the Bell system.

Normally a large number of organizations of the relevant order are exposed to an innovative idea and, as a consequence, must unilaterally determine the significance of the idea for their operations as well as for the community at large. Out of these determinations some type of interorganizational action invariably occurs.

Studies of development efforts in Michigan's Upper Peninsula provide empirical evidence that interorganizational coupling does occur in very systematic ways both within and across social, economic, political, and geographic interest sectors (Anderson 1963, 1976; and Chapter 10). Sociometric findings showed the existence of 21 constellation sets—highly selective groups of organizations expressing reciprocal dependency relationships—within 11 economic interest sectors in 14 geographic regions.

Organization goals and goal structures are obvious critical factors accounting for why organizations normally interact with each other. This seems to be particularly true when it comes to the adoption of innovative ideas. To test this notion the sociometric data were reexamined using Etzioni's (1975) organization goal classification typology. All of the 61 organizations representing 11 different economic interest sectors could be easily classified using this system. Under this system, an organization goal is a state of affairs the organization is attempting to realize. It is an image of a future state of the organization (Parsons 1937). It is an organizational variable that can be empirically determined and as such is subject to systematic classification. The three types of organizational goals used to classify all organizations are defined as follows:

* Organizations with *ordered goals* attempt to prevent the occurrence of specific events and to ensure the occurrence of other goals which are considered normative to the larger system. Their mission is to control actors (organizations as well as individuals) who are perceived as deviants by society at large.

* Organizations with *economic goals* attempt to produce or to make available commodities and services for rent or sale to other organizations or individuals within the society at large on a nonprofit as well as a profit basis.

* Organizations with *cultural goals* attempt to institutionalize conditions necessary for the creation, application, and preservation of symbolic objects, belief systems, and value orientations within society at large.

While every organization may, at one time or another, exhibit all these goal characteristics when classified in relation to a specific idea, the goal state of highest priority for each organization should determine what classification is assigned to it.

The sociometric data from the Upper Peninsula study clearly identified organizations within given coalition sets from each of the three goal classification categories. Such findings not only lend credence to the utility of the goal classification scheme, they also provide evidence to support the following hypothesis on how innovative ideas are implemented at the community level, for the organizations in this study were identified both by reputation and actual events as major forces in the economic development of Michigan's U.P. (Anderson 1963, 1976).

HYPOTHESIS:
For an innovative idea to be implemented at the community level, at least three organizations from the relevant order, with at least one from each of the three kinds of community organizations—ordered, economic, and cultural—must couple and jointly commit their independent organizational resources to support the idea before it will be implemented at the community level.

Failure to meet this minimum requirement leads to the following alternatives:

* The rejection and abandonment of the idea.

* The modification of the idea in a manner to merit support and adoption by sufficient numbers of organizations from the relevant order to implement the idea. This process may be repeated several times before adoption occurs.

* A differentiation of the community structure and the emergence of a community conflict situation. The outcome

may be: the adoption of the idea, modification of the idea and its adoption, or the rejection of the idea.

Despite these seemingly impossible conditions, only a few organizations in the relevant order need to adopt and commit resources in support of the idea for the innovation to be implemented. When implemented, it becomes part of the normative structure of the community to which all other organizational members of the community accommodate.

Figure 23 illustrates the configuration of organizations making up the relevant order for a given innovative idea. They are shown as distributions of organizations as classified by Etzioni's goal typology (defined above). Note that in any given situation the largest number of organizations will be classified as economic goal type organizations, a smaller number as ordered goal-type organizations, and cultural goal-type organizations will make up the smallest group. All organizations in the relevant order unilaterally determine the merit of the idea. Each organization, given its economic, political, and social situation at the time, will make a judgment about the idea in terms of positive or negatives with intensities ranging from low to high. The judgment determines the position each organization will take with respect to the idea. They will support or reject it depending upon the value and intensity of their judgment. (See Chapter 6, Figure 5.)

A few organizations at the high-intensity level will actively commit resources either in support of (a positive value) or in opposition to (a negative value) implementation efforts. In most cases, however, a large majority of all organizations within the relevant order will take a position of indifference to the idea; they will not commit resources either in support of or in opposition to the idea. Rather they will accommodate and use the idea after the early adopters have demonstrated its merits. Note the small number of organizations in the shaded areas of Figure 25. These are the organizations that, because of the high intensity related to their judgment of the ideas engage in coupling activities with other organizations either to fight or support the implementation of the idea at the community level.

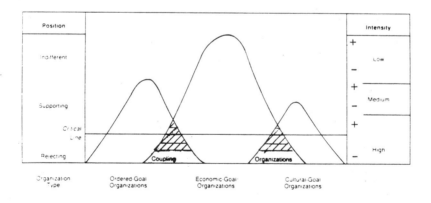

Figure 23. *Involvement patterns of relevant order organizations in the implementation of an innovative idea at the community level*

The coupling organizations in the shaded area above the critical line in Figure 23 represent a sufficient and necessary population to cause the implementation of the innovative idea, provided that in their ranks there is at least one ordered organization, one economic organization, and one cultural organization in the distribution. Coupling organizations in the shaded area below the critical line represent a sufficient but not necessary population to cause non implementation of the idea regardless of their goal typology. Non coupling organizations, represented in the unshaded area of the figure, will no doubt adopt the innovation once it has been successfully implemented by the early adopting organizations.

The *coupling process* is a dynamic succession or series of interorganizational communications at the community level in which the purpose, content, and structure required for implementation of an idea are proposed, tested, adjusted, and negotiated until convergence and agreement toward the end purpose of the process is reached. Coupling organizations are drawn into this communication stage through many and varied mechanisms. Individuals may initiate the process, an organization or individual may refer the idea to others, organizations may seek each other out as a result of newspaper, radio, or TV coverage of the idea. However this happens, the coupling and communication process takes place at the community level at the time the idea emerges in the community. For the most part, participants meet and engage each other on the battlefield as the struggle to implement the idea takes place.

The implementation of the innovative idea in the community is achieved when sufficient interorganizational links are in place, coupled, and tied together to overcome the resistance of opposing organizations.

A Case in Point

In December 1985, the City Council of East Lansing, Michigan, passed an ordinance banning smoking in public places. This ordinance is used to illustrate that the coupling of organized interests does happen when innovative change occurs at the community level. It serves as a case study that lends support to the hypotheses of the number and kinds of organizations needed to secure the adoption of an innovative idea.

In this case, the city council, an *ordered goal-type organization,* after much tugging and hauling, passed and implemented a "no smoking in public places" ordinance with relatively strong enforcement provisions.

Travel, retail sales, restaurant, and bar establishments, representing the *economic goal-type organizations* of the city, split badly on the issue. Most committed resources to defeat the proposed ordinance, as they believed it would do serious harm to their business and was a violation of the rights of customers and employees who smoked. However, one or two commercial organizations did support the non-smoking ordinance and committed resources to that support.

Cultural goal-type organizations, such as the American Lung Association, the American Heart Association, the American Cancer Society, the county medical society, the state, regional, and local chambers of commerce, the Tobacco Trade Association of Michigan, and the American Tobacco Institute also became very involved in the process. The health-related organizations committed resources in support of the innovation. The chambers of commerce considered the idea to be frivolous and hoped it would go away, but offered no serious resistance. The tobacco institute spent much effort to discredit and defeat the ordinance with the argument that it was an "unwarranted intrusion in the workplace."

In this case, more than 35 committed organizations, at least one representing each of the three kinds of community organizations— ordered, economic, and cultural goal types—did couple and commit their respective organizational resources in support of an ordinance prohibiting smoking in public places in the city of East Lansing. They achieved an innovative change in the way business is now carried out in the city.

Obviously, time and contemporary conditions impinge on each organization that becomes drawn into such interorganizational activities. It is useful in the understanding and use of the theory to examine how individual organizations are likely to react when faced with a situation in which they may or may not become actively involved in the adoption of an innovative idea at the community level.

Relationships between Organizations Classified by Goals and the Organizational Conditions Favorable for the Adoption of Innovative Ideas

Organizations tend to be more receptive to the adoption of innovative ideas early in their life cycle. This is understandable as innovation is the general reason new organizations are created (Kimberly et al. 1980). But the process of adopting and institutionalizing innovative ideas is an ongoing function in most, if not all, established organizations as well. Organizations of all kinds must deal with ideas that are worthy of adoption and implementation. Conditions favorable for this to occur during an organization's life span may be accounted for on a continuum from a state of irreplaceable loss to a state of surplus energy (see Figure 24).

	Conditions Favorable for Adoption		
Kinds of Organizations Classified by Goals	Irreplaceable Loss	Planned Change	Surplus Energy
Ordered-goal Economic-goal Cultural-goal	type 1 (- -) type 4 (0 -) type 7 (0 0)	type 2 (0 -) type 5 (0 ±) type 8 (0 +)	type 3 (0 0) type 6 (0 +) type 9 (+ +)

0 -	=	a low-intensity negative condition
- -	=	an intense negative condition
0 0	=	a low-intensity nondirection condition
0 +	=	a low-intensity positive condition
+ +	=	an intense positive or negative condition
0 ±	=	a low-intensity positive or negative condition

Figure 24. *Typologies of conditions for organizational adoption relationships*

An organization's willingness, and even its perception of the necessity, to adopt innovative ideas is paramount at a time of irreplaceable organizational loss, that is, the loss of familiar attachments and understandings that represent the purposes and meaning in an organization's life (Marris 1974). Organizations, like individuals, react to a "bereavable" or irreplaceable loss, first with numbness and ambivalence, followed by an impulse to replace and restore the loss in its original form. When replacement is found to be impossible, grief, anger, and internal conflict boil over. An internal crisis of reintegration emerges that must be worked out among the members of that organization alone. At this point, any outside effort to preempt the conflict by minimizing the argument or rational planning can only be abortive. The process of reintegration must allow the first impulse of rejection to play itself out.

During the process of organizational grieving, adaptive will and abilities emerge and the organization survives the crisis by accepting the loss and moving forward with innovative accommodation to its new situation. At this point in the life cycle of many organizations, the very survival of the organization depends upon the emergence of such an adaptive condition. An organization in this condition will seek changes that predictably will place it in an environment that is tolerable both internally and socially. Marris (1974, 91) has pointed out that "the management of change depends on our ability to articulate the process of grieving. Without this sensitivity to the implications of loss, any conception of change becomes callously destructive."

The continuum of conditions sufficient for an organization to adopt innovative ideas moves to the concept of *planned change*—a method by which an organization consciously and experimentally employs knowledge to help solve organizational problems (Dennis et al. 1976). This is a logical rational process based in part on the scientific method, but also grounded in philosophical concepts of "goodness" as represented in personal, political, organizational, religious, and cultural values of society. Morton (1971) argues that innovation through the planned change condition is an adaptive change of the existing organization, the means that many organizations use to achieve organizational renewal. An idea, group of ideas, or knowledge, is an essential ingredient to the process. Our knowledge system is so large and complex today that no one can master the understanding of all levels. To be creative, we must specialize and then, in Morton's terminology, combine knowledge from many sources for understanding and synthesis by the larger system.

The planned change type of innovative process is a repeated application of the scientific method. It is a flexible, adaptive activity in which, for each area of knowledge specialization, forward and feedback communication links within and between organizational units are formed to propose, test, modify, and retest ideas until a concept emerges that is meritorious enough to command support within the organization's decision-making structure.

For planned change types of innovations to occur within an organization, the organization must have and implement an innovation policy. It must have (and most organizations do) organizational strategies for achieving major organizational renewal objectives.

Zaltman et al. (1973) refer to planned change type of innovation as *programmed innovation;* that is, a strategy that provides for advanced scheduling with defined procedures and routines established to evaluate and implement innovative ideas that pass the organizational tests. They note that organizational success in ongoing operations, high-quality managerial expertise, technological know-how, financial, social, structural, and procedural flexibility, and a willingness to take risks are all necessary attributes of an organization before preplanned adoption of an innovative idea can occur.

To program innovation into an organization is to accept organizational risk and uncertainty in the belief that such a strategy is necessary for the long-term viability of the organization. The greater the degree of programmed innovation within an organization over time, the less predictable and logical the organizational behavior will be. Programmed innovation can and does occur within subunits of the organization, within the organization as a whole, and in many cases in cooperation with one or more independent organizations.

Probably the most interesting and theoretically the most ideal period in the life cycle of organizations for the adoption of innovative ideas is the period of *surplus energy.* This condition, often referred to as *organizational slack,* occurs when resources are relatively unlimited. Slack-type innovations (March and Simon 1959; Zaltman et al. 1973) are not the result of the need to survive, an irreplaceable loss, or programmed innovation. They are simply serendipitous, or the products of affluence.

The invention and adoption of the automobile is an example of surplus energy innovation. No one really wanted the automobile to solve a pressing transportation or, for that matter, any other kind of problem; it didn't replace an irreplaceable loss; it wasn't even a product of a research and development unit. Some tinkerers in the buggy manufacturing business with surplus energy simply put engines on buggies, and, despite the objection of horses and their owners, the idea caught on. More recently, human exploration on the moon, the space walks, and in-space satellite repair are a result of national and international slack rather than of basic survival needs. Because of national affluence, it became acceptable to join the dreamers in space adventures.

Slack or nonprogrammed innovations need not resolve the relative merits of subgroup claims or any other claims. The rationalizations or justification for these innovations tend not to be challenged within the organization. Rather, substantial differentiation of organizational goals and structure occurs. No initial threat or expense, perceived or otherwise, to the subgroups of the organization or to other organizations in the larger social order is felt. Such innovations do, of course, potentially represent substantial risk, uncertainty, and discontinuity to the organization and society at large. But because, at the time, the resource base is unrestricted, the organization can and does afford such risk, and society generally humors and tolerates such innovative efforts.

Within the framework shown in Figure 24, the two variables—the *kinds of goals* an organization has and the *conditions present* that are favorable for the adoption of an innovative idea—constitute the relationships likely to be present when an organization adopts an innovation. That is, an organization with ordered goals is more likely to adopt an innovative idea when it has experienced an irreplaceable loss (type 1). Organizations with utilitarian goals are more likely to adopt innovative ideas emerging from programmed or planned change conditions (type 5). And organizations with predominantly cultural goals are more likely to adopt innovative ideas under conditions of surplus energy or conditions of organizational slack (type 9).

It is hypothesized that innovation types 1, 5, and 9 will occur most frequently, are theoretically more effective, and should be considered congruent relationships. Most organizations, regardless of goal type, will at one time or another in their life cycle experience the condition of irreplaceable loss or surplus resources. Under either condition, organizations are more likely to be receptive to the adoption of innovative ideas. Types 2, 3, 4, 6, 7, and 8 are considered to be incongruent types; they may occur frequently but they are considered to be less effective as a condition for innovation.

As a practical matter, most organizations for most of their life cycle tend to find themselves somewhere between the points of irreplaceable loss or surplus energy. It is not uncommon to find conditions represented in Figure 24 as types 2, 3, 4, 6, 7, and 8, which are considered to be incongruent types. A shift from an incongruent to a congruent situation may be attained either by changing the goals of the organization or the conditions favorable for the adoption of innovations.

The Relationship between Power Used and the Adoption Orientation of Members to Innovative Ideas

Organizations must adopt new ideas continually if they are to survive. This must be done while maintaining a level of traditional operation sufficient to sustain organizational life. Both functions require the exercise of power and orientation toward compliance by organizational members as well as the larger social system to the exercise of this power.

Etzioni (1975) provides a classification scheme useful to the study of the interorganizational variables: organizational power, involvement, and compliance. These theoretical constructs are used here to analyze adoption of innovative ideas by organizations. Power refers to an organization's ability to induce or influence its members to carry out organizational directions and any other norm supported by the organization. Compliance refers both to a relation in which an actor behaves in accordance with a directive supported by another actor's power and the orientation of the subordinated actor to the power applied.

Within this framework, two variables—*the kind of power applied by the organization to its members,* and *the orientations of members to* the power used to secure implementation of the adopted innovative idea—structure the compliance relationships likely to occur when innovation is adopted and implemented by the organization. It produces nine types of compliance as shown in Figure 25.

The phrase adoption orientations means the evaluative orientation of organization members and subgroups to the adoption by the organization of an innovative idea. The orientations are characterized in terms of intensity and direction (similar to Etzioni's definition of involvement). The typology is presented as a continuum with alienative designating intense negative orientations, calculative designating low-intensity negative or positive orientations, and moral designating highly intensive positive orientations of the organization members as they comply and implement the innovative idea as adopted.

Kinds of Orientations to Adoption			
Kinds of Power Used	Alienative	Calculative	Moral
Coercive	type 1 (- -)	type 2 (0 -)	type 3 (0 0)
Remunerative	type 4 (0 -)	type 5 (0 ±)	type 6 (0 +)
Normative	type 7 (0 0)	type 8 (0 +)	type 9 (+ +)

0 -	=	a low-intensity negative orientation
- -	=	intense negative orientation
0 0	=	a low-intensity nondirectional orientation
0 +	=	a low-intensity positive orientation
+ +	=	intense positive orientation
0 +	=	a low-intensity negative or positive orientation

Figure 25.   Typologies of compliance relations of members to the adoption of an innovative idea

The power continuum includes *coercive* power—the threat or actual application of physical sanctions by the organization so as to inflict pain, discomfort, deformity, or death; *remunerative* power—the control and allocation of the organization's material resources, rewards, and sanctions; and *normative* power—the allocation and manipulation by the organization of symbolic rewards and deprivations.

In Figure 25 we see that the use of coercive power by an organization will result in intensely negative member and subgroup orientations to the idea as it is implemented (type 1). Use of remunerative power will result in either low intensity negative or positive member and subgroup orientations to the implementation of the idea (type 5). The use of normative power will result in positive member and subgroup orientation of high intensity around the implementation of an innovative idea (type 9). Types 1, 5, and 9 occur most often and are theoretically more effective uses of power to achieve member compliance to the adoption of an innovative idea. As such, they are considered to be congruent relationships.

Every organization, at one time or another, will use all three kinds of power in various combinations (depending upon the operation at hand) in order to get member compliance. The other six types will be used occasionally. Because they are theoretically less effective, types 2, 3, 4, 6, and 8 are considered to be incongruent. Since congruent-type compliance relationships are theoretically more effective, they are also more desirable. Congruence may be attained by changing either the kind of power applied by the organization or the orientation of members and subgroups to the innovative idea itself.

Summary and Conclusion

In this chapter I have identified organizational and interorganizational factors (i.e., organizational goal types, conditions, and power used to secure member compliance) that account for and help explain the adoption and implementation of innovative ideas at the community level. General models of how innovative ideas are dealt with by organizations and how organizations couple to implement these ideas are presented. The adoption and implementation of innovative ideas were chosen because they represent a much more complex and difficult change process than do other more normative and everyday types of change activities. However, normative planned change activities also are accounted for with this work.

If the theory and models presented here turn out to have validity when submitted to repeated rigorous validation testing, we will have created yet another tool with which to plan and carry out community change activities. When using this tool, community change agents should be in a better position to develop more effective change strategies and procedures by which to make our communities better places in which to live.

This interorganizational approach to community change should not in any way be perceived as an effort to displace or discredit other more traditional and person-oriented community change models. Rather, it is my hope that what is presented here will serve to supplement and extend the utility of the wide array of community change models that are documented in our political, economic, community development, social work, and sociological literature.

BIBLIOGRAPHY

Aboulafia, Mitchell, ed.
1991   *Philosophy, Social Theory, and Thought of George Herbert Mead*. Albany: State University of New York Press.

Aldrich, Howard E.
1979   *Organizations and Environments*. Englewood Cliffs, New Jersey: Prentice-Hall Inc.

Anderson, Robert C.
1963   *A Method and Instrument for Predicting the Consequences of Intraorganizational Action*. Unpublished Ph.D. dissertation, Michigan State University, East Lansing, MI.

1963   "The Perceived Organized Structure of Michigan's Upper Peninsula." East Lansing: Michigan State University, Department of Sociology, research report.

1964   "The Development Organization Concept of Organization for Inventiveness: An Interorganizational Approach to Development." East Lansing: Michigan State University, Department of Sociology, research report.

1968   "Community Cooperation and Involvement." In *The Community: What Is It?* Proceedings of the Conference on Human Relations, Institute for Community Development and Services, Michigan State University, East Lansing, MI. May 4, 1968.

1970   "Our Educational Model of Participation Examined."
             Journal of the Community Development Society 1, no. 2
             (Fall):79-88.

1976   "A Sociometric Approach to the Analysis of Interorganiza-
             tional Relations." In *Interorganizational Relations*, edited by
             William M. Evans. New York: Penguin.

1986   "An Interorganizational Approach to the Explanation of
             Community Development Activities." *Clinical Sociology
             Review* 4:71-90.

1990   "A Technique for Predicting Intraorganizational Action."
             Clinical Sociology Review 8:128-142.

1990   "Community Cooperation and Development." *Sociological
             Practice* 8:133 -144.

Anderson, Robert C., and Nancy Gendell
1981   "Community Development as a University Outreach
             Function." In *New Directions for Continuing Education:
             Continuing Education for Community Leadership*, edited by
             Harold W. Stubblefield. San Francisco: Jossey-Bass.

Andrew, Gwen
1958   *Principles of Perception.* New York: Harper and Bros.

1961   *Criteria for Systems Models and Their Application to a
             Sociological Theory of Organizations.* Unpublished Ph.D.
             dissertation, Michigan State University, East Lansing, MI.

Andrews, David
1984   *The IRG Solution: Hierarchial Incompetence and How to
             Overcome It.* London: Souvenir Press Ltd.

Backarach, Samuel B., and Edward J. Lawler
1980   *Power and Politics in Organizations.*   San Francisco:
             Jossey-Bass.

Barnard, Chester I.
1938   *The Functions of the Executive.* Cambridge: Harvard
        University Press.

Bartley, Howard S.
1958   *Principles of Perception.* New York: Harper and Bros.

Bassis, Michael S., Richard J. Gelles, and Ann Levine
1980   *Sociology: An Introduction.* New York: Random House.

Belshaw, Cyril S.
1970   *The Conditions of Social Performance: An Exploratory
        Theory.* New York: Schocken Books.

Bettleheim, Bruno
1974   *A Home for the Heart.* London: Thames and Hudson.

Bidwell, Charles E., and John D. Kasarda
1987   *Structuring in Organizations: Ecosystem Theory Evaluated.*
        Greenwich: Jai Press, Inc.

1991   *Biosphere 2: A World of Discovery.* Tucson: Bio 2.

Bloomberg, Warner, Jr., and Florence W. Rostenstock
1968   "Who Can Activate the Poor? One Assessment of 'Maxi-
        mum Feasible Participation'." In *Power, Poverty, and Urban
        Policy*, edited by Warner Bloomberg, Jr. and Henry J.
        Schmandt. Beverly Hills: Sage Publications.

Boulding, Kenneth
1961   *The Image.* Ann Arbor: The University of Michigan Press.

Boyer, Ernest L.
1990   *Scholarship Reconsidered: Priorities of the Professorate.*
        New Jersey: The Carnegie Foundation for the Advance-
        ment of Teaching.

Bratkovich, Jerrold R., Bernadette Steele, and Garry N. Teesdale
1989   "The Reward System as a Tool for Reinforcing Innovation
            and Entrepreneurial Behavior." In *Human Resources
            Strategies for Organizations in Transition*, edited by Richard
            J. Niehaus and Karl F. Price. New York: Plenum Press.

Britan, Gerald M., and Ronald Cohen, eds.
1980   *Hierarchy and Society: Anthropological Perspectives on
            Bureaucracy*. Philadelphia (PA) Institute for the Study of
            Human Issues.

Bryant, Christopher G. A., and David Jary, eds.
1991   *Gidden's Theory of Structuration: A Critical Appreciation*.
            London: Routledge.

Burns, Tom R., and Helena Flam
1987   *The Shaping of Social Organization: Social Rule System
            Theory With Applications*. Beverly Hills: Sage Publications.

Burns, Tom, and G. M. Stalker.
1961   *The Management of Innovation*. Chicago: Quadrangle
            Books.

Cahn, Edgar S., and Jean Camper Cahn
1968   "Citizen Participation." In *Citizen Participation in Urban
            Development, Vol. 1—Concepts and Issues*, edited by Hans
            B.C. Spiegel. Washington, DC: NTL Institute for Applied
            Behavioral Science.

Chekki, Dan A., ed.
1990   *Research in Community Studies*, vol 1.   Greenwich: Jai
            Press Inc.

Ciciotti, E., N. Alderman, and A. Thwaites
1990   *Technological Changes in a Spatial Context*. Berlin: Verlag.

Clark, Phil Jon, Cetia Modgil, and Sohan Modgil, eds.
1990   *Robert K. Merton, Consensus and Controversy*. London:
            Falmer Press.

Corwin, Ronald G.
1987   *The Organization—Society Nexus: A Critical Review of Models and Metaphors.* New York: Greenwood Press.

Crain, Robert L., and Donald B. Rosenthal
1967   "Community Status as a Dimension of Local Decision Making." *American Sociological Review* 32:970-984.

Dahl, Robert A.
1961   *Who Governs?* New Haven: Yale University Press.

D'Antonio, William V., and Eugene C. Erickson
1962   "The Reputational Technique as a Measure of Community Power: An Evaluation Based on Comparative and Longitudinal Studies." *American Sociological Review* 27 (June): 362-376.

Dennis, Warren G., et al., ed.
1976   *The Planning of Change*, 3rd edition. New York: Holt, Rinehart and Winston.

de Tocqueville, Alexis
1945   "Associations in American Life." *Democracy in America.* Trans. by Phillips Bradley. New York: Alfred A. Knopf, Inc.

1960   *Democracy in America* (1835), vol 1. New York: Vintage Books, Inc.

Deutsch, Morton
1990   "Cooperation, Conflict, and Justice." In *Advances in Field Theory,* edited by Susan A. Wheelan, Emmy A. Pepitone, and Vicki Abt. Newbury Park: Sage Publications.

Dirrell, Fletcher
1936   *Cooperation, Essence and Background.* Cape Mercy Court House, NJ: Gazette Print Shop.

Dunlop, John T., ed.
1962   *Automation and Technological Change.* Englewood Cliffs,
            NJ: Prentice-Hall, Inc.

Edelston, Harold C., and Ferne K. Kolodner
1968   "Are the Poor Capable of Planning for Themselves?" In
            *Citizen Participation in Urban Development, Vol. 1—
            Concepts and Issues,* edited by Hans B.C. Spiegel. Wash-
            ington DC: NTL Institute for Applied Behavioral Science

Edwards, Allen, and Dorothy G. Jones
1976   *Community and Community Development.* The Hague:
            Mouton Publishers.

Effrat, Marcia Pelly, ed.
1974   *The Community: Approaches and Applications.* New York:
            The Free Press.

Emmerich, Herbert
1978   "Bureaucracy in America: Some Personal Reflections." In
            Society and History, edited by G. L. Ulmen. The Hague:
            Mouton Publishers.

Etzioni, Amitai
1961   *A Comparative Analysis of Complex Organizations.* New
            York: The Free Press.

1964   *Complex Organizations: A Sociological Reader.*   New
            York: Holt, Rinehart and Winston.

1975   *A Comparative Analysis of Complex Organizations,* revised
            edition. New York: The Free Press.

Eva, William A.
1966   "The Organization-Set: Toward a Theory of Interorganiza-
            tional Relations." In *Approaches to Organizational Design,*
            edited by James D. Thompson. Pittsburgh: University of
            Pittsburgh Press.

Galbraith, John K.
1967   *The New Industrial State*. Boston: Houghton Mifflin Co.

Galaskiewicz, Z. Joseph
1979   *Exchange Networks and Community Politics*. Beverly Hills: Sage Publications.

Gardner, Lindzey, and Donn Byrne, eds.
1968   "Measurement of Social Choice and Interpersonal Attractiveness." In *The Handbook of Social Psychology*, vol. 2, 2nd edition, edited by Lindzey Gardner and Elliot Aronson. Reading, MA: Addison-Wesley Publishers.

Golembiewski, Robert F.
1968   "Integrating Small Behavioral Units into Large Formal Organizations." In *People, Groups, and Organizations*, edited by Bernard P. Indik and F. Kenneth Berrin. New York: Teachers College Press.

Gouldner, Alvin W.
1959   "Organization Analysis." In *Sociology Today*, edited by Robert K. Merton, Leonard Broom, Leonard S. Cottrell Jr. New York: Basic Books.

Gray, Barbara
1989   *Collaborating: Finding Ground for Multiparty Problems*. San Francisco: Jossey-Bass.

Gronbjerg, Kirsten A.
1989   "Communities and Nonprofit Organizations: Interlocking Ecological Systems." In *Dimensions of Communities: A Research Handbook*, edited by Dan A. Chekki. New York: Garland Publishing Inc.

Gross, Neal, Ward Mason, and Alexander N. McEachern
1958   *Exploration in Role Analysis*. New York: John Wiley and Sons.

Gusfield, Joseph R.
1975   *Community: A Critical Response*. New York: Harper and
            Row Publishers.

Haas, J. Eugene, and Thomas E. Drabek
1973   *Complex Organizations: A Sociological Perspective*. New
            York: The Macmillan Company.

Hall, Richard H.
1987   *Organization Structures, Processes, and Outcomes*, 4th
            edition. Englewood Cliffs: Prentice-Hall Inc.

Hawley, Amos H.
1950   *Human Ecology: A Theory of Community Structure*. New
            York: The Ronald Press.

Heady, Earl O., and Harold R. Jensen
1957   "The Field of Farm Management." In *Farm Management
            Economics*. New York: Prentice-Hall Inc.

Hempel, C., and P. Oppenheim
1953   "The Logic of Explanation." In *Readings in the Philosophy
            of Science*, edited by H. Fiegl and M. Brodbeck. New York:
            Appleton-Century-Crofts, Inc.

Holt, Carolyn D.
1989   "Making Entrepreneuring Happen: Organizational Tools and
            Processes for New Business Development." In *Human
            Resources Strategies for Organizations in Transition*, edited
            by Richard J. Niehaus and Karl F. Price. New York: Plenum
            Press.

Horgan, John
1992   "Quantum Philsophy." *Scientific American* 267:94-95.

Huey, Jon
1991   *Tenure For Socrates: A Study in the Betrayal of the
            American Professor*. New York: Bergin and Garvey.

Hunter, Floyd
1959   *Community Power Structure.* Chapel Hill: University of
            North Carolina Press.

1959   *Top Leadership.* Chapel Hill: University of North Carolina
            Press.

1990   *Jane's Publications.*   London: Macdonald and Jane's
            Publishing Co.

Kahh, Robert L., and Mayer N. Zald, eds.
1990   *Organization and Nation-States: New Perspectives on
            Conflict and Cooperation.* San Francisco: Jossey-Bass

Kanter, Rosabeth Moss
1983   *The Change Masters.* New York: Simon and Schuster.

Kelman, Herbert C., and Donald P. Warwick
1973   "Bridging Micro and Macro Approaches to Social Change:
            A Social-psychological Perspective."   In *Processes and
            Phenomena of Social Change*, edited by Gerald Zaltman.
            New York: John Wiley and Sons, Inc.

Kimberly, John R., Robert H. Miles, and associates
1980   *The Organizational Life Cycle.* San Francisco: Jossey-Bass.

Kish, Leslie
1953   "Selection of the Sample." In *Research Methods in the
            Behavioral Sciences*, edited by Leon Festinger and Daniel
            Katz. New York: The Dryden Press.

Kuhn, Manford H., and Thomas S. MacPortland
1954   "An Empirical Investigation of Self-Attitudes." In *American
            Sociological Review: The Manual for the Twenty-State-
            ment Problem.* Kansas City, MO: The Greater Kansas City
            Mental Health Foundation.

Lee, Robert, L. Craig, and Donald B. Rosenthal
1967   "Community Status as a Dimension of Local Decision-Making." *American Sociological Review* 32:970-984.

Levine, Joel H.
1972   "The Sphere of Influence." *American Sociological Review* 37:14-27.

Levy Jr., Marion J.
1966   *Modernization and the Structure of Societies.* Princeton: Princeton University Press.

Likert, Rensis
1961   *New Patterns of Management.* New York: McGraw-Hill.

Lingoes, J.C., and Edward E. Roskan
1973   *"A Mathematical and Empirical Analysis of Two Multi-Dimensional Scaling Algorithms. "* Psychometrics 19:74-76.

Litwak, Eugene, and Lydia F. Hylton
1962   "Inter-organizational Analysis: A Hypothesis on Coordinating Agencies." *Administrative Science Quarterly* 6, no. 4:240-395.

Long, Huey B., Robert C. Anderson, and Jon A. Blubaugh, eds.
1973   *Approaches to Community Development.* Iowa City: National University Extension Association and the American College Testing Program.

Loomis, C. P.
1960   *Social Systems: Essays on Their Persistance and Change.* Princeton: Van Nostrand.

Loumann, Edward C., and Franz U. Pappi
1976   *Networks of Collective Action.* New York: Academic Press.

Lozano, Eduardo E.
1990   *Community Design and the Culture of Cities.* Cambridge: Cambridge University Press.

Lundstedt, Sven B., ed.
1990   *Telecommunications, Values, and the Public Interest.* New Jersey: Ablex Publications.

Makken, Robert J.
1985   "Legislative Analysis: Methodology for the Analysis of Groups and Coalitions." In *Coalition Formation*, edited by Henki A.M. Wilke. Amsterdam: Elsevier Science Publ.

March, James G., ed.
1965   *Handbook of Organizations.* Chicago: Rand McNally.

March, James G., and Herbert A. Simon
1959   *Organizations.* New York: John Wiley and Sons, Inc.

Marris, Peter
1974   *Loss and Change.* London: Routledge and Kegan Paul.

Matejko, Alexander J.
1986   *In Search of New Organizational Paradigms.* New York: Praeger.

Mead, G. H.
1934   *Mind, Self, and Society: From the Standpoint of a Social Behaviorist.* Chicago: University of Chicago Press.

Merton, Robert K.
1957   *Social Theory and Social Structure.* Glencoe, IL: The Free Press.

Merton, Robert K., L. Broom, and L.S. Cottrell, Jr., eds.
1959   *Sociology Today.* New York: Basic Books.

Meyer, John W., and W. Richard Scott
1983   *Organizational Environments: Ritual and Rationality.* Beverly Hills: Sage Publications.

Miller, Paul A.
1952   "The Process of Decision Making: the Center of Community
            Organization." *Rural Sociology* 2 (June):153-161.

1953   *Community Health Action: A Study of Community
            Contrast.* East Lansing: Michigan State College Press.

Misra, Bhabagrahi, and James Preston eds.
1978   *Community, Self and Identity.* The Hague: Mouton Publ.

Mitroff, Ian I., and Thierry C. Tauchant
1990   *We're So Big and Powerful Nothing Bad Can Happen to Us.*
            Secaucus: Carol Publishing Group.

Moe, Edward O.
1959   "Consulting with a Community System: A Case Study."
            Journal of Social Issues XV, no. 2:25.

Morgan, Arthur E.
1957   *The Community of the Future.* Yellow Springs, OH: Antioch
            College.

Morton, J.A.
1971   *Organizing for Innovation.* New York: McGraw-Hill.

Mysior, Arnold
1977   *Society—A Very Large System: A Systems-Theoretic
            Approach to the Study of Society.* Washington, DC:
            University Press of America.

Negandhi, Anant R.
1975   *Organization Theory in an Open System.* New York:
            Dunellen Publishers.

Newman, Oscar
1981   *Community of Interest.* Garden City: Anchor Press.

Niehaus, Richard J., and Karl F. Price, eds.
1989   *Human Resources Strategies for Organizations in Transition.* New York: Plenum Press.

Nixon, Wilfred J., and Frank J. Massey, Jr.
1957   *Introduction to Statistical Analysis.* New York: McGraw-Hill.

Parsons, Talcott
1937   *The Structure of Social Action.* New York: McGraw-Hill.

1956   "Suggestions for a Sociological Approach to a Theory of Organizations." *Administrative Science Quarterly* 1 (June):63-85 amd 2 (September):225-239.

1960   *The Structure and Process in Modern Societies.* Glencoe, IL: The Free Press.

Plant, Raymond
1974   *Community and Ideology: An Essay on Applied Social Philosophy.* London: Routledge and Kegan Paul.

Popenoe, David
1968   "The Social Culture Context of People, Groups, and Organizations." In *People, Groups, and Organizations,* edited by Bernard P. Indik and F. Kenneth Berrien. New York: Teachers College Press.

Poplin, Dennis E.
1972   *Communities: A Survey of Theories and Methods of Research.* New York: Macmillan Publ. Co.

1979   *Communities,* 2nd edition. New York: Macmillan Publ. Co.

Presthus, Robert
1978   *The Organizational Society,* revised edition. New York: St. Martin's Press.

Reichers, Arnon E., and Benjamin Schneider
1990   "Climate and Culture: An Evolution of Constructs."   In
            Organizational, Climate and Culture, edited by Benjamin
            Schneider. San Francisco: Jossey-Bass.

Roberts, Hayden
1979   *Community Development: Learning and Actions*. Toronto:
            University of Toronto Press.

Rogers, Everett M.
1975   "Where We Are in Understanding the Diffusion of Innova-
            tions." Paper presented at *Communication and Change:
            Ten Years after Honolulu*, the East-West Communication
            Institute Conference.

1983   *Diffusion of Innovations*, 3rd edition. New York: The Free
            Press.

Rogers Everett M., and Rekhja Agarwala-Rogers
1976   *Communications in Organizations*, 3rd edition. Glencoe, IL:
            The Free Press.

Rogers, Everett M., et al.
1969   *Diffusion of Innovations, Educational Changes in Thai
            Government Secondary Schools*. East Lansing, MI: Insti-
            tute for Interrelational Studies in Education and Department
            of Communications report.

Rothman, Jack
1980   *Using Research in Organizations: A Guide to Successful
            Applications*. Beverly Hills: Sage Publications.

Rothman, Jack, John L. Erlich, and Joseph G. Teresa
1981   *Changing Organizations and Community Programs*. Beverly
            Hills: Sage Publications.

Sanders, Irwin T.
1972   *The Community: An Introduction to a Social System*, 2nd
            edition. New York: The Ronald Press.

Scherer, Jacqueline
1972   *Contemporary Community: Sociological Illusion or Reality?*
            London: Tavistock Publications.

Schmitt, Donna M., and Donald C. Weaver
1979   *Leadership for Community Empowerment: A Source Book.*
            Midland: Pendell Publishing Comapny.

Schneider, Benjamin, ed.
1990   *Organizational Climate and Culture.* San Francisco: Jossey-
            Bass.

Schwartz, Howard S.
1990   *Narcissistic Process and Corporate Decay: The Theory of
            the Organizational Ideal.* New York: New York University
            Press.

Sills, David L.
1957   *Joining the Foundation, the Volunteers: Means and Ends
            in a National Organization.* Glencoe, IL: The Free Press.

Silverman, Carol J., and Steven E. Baston
1989   "Common Interest Communities and the American Dream."
            In *Dimensions of Community: A Research Handbook*, edited
            by Dan A. Chekki. New York: Garland Publishing, Inc.

Simon, Herbert A.
1964   "On the Concept of Organizational Goals." *Administrative
            Science Quarterly* 9, no. 1:1-22.

Snygg, Donald, and Arthur W. Combs
1949   *Individual Behavior.* New York: Harper and Bros.

Sower, Christopher
1957   "The Land Grant University 'Development Organization' in Transition: The Case of the Cooperative Service." In *Proceedings of Seventh Annual Cooperative Administrative Seminar*. Madison, WI: University of Wisconsin, Extension Center for Advanced Study.

Sower, Christopher, Robert Hanson, David Westby, and Norbert Wiley
1962   "The Roles of Organizations in Achieving the Goals of Planned Change." *Highway and Locality Change*. East Lansing, MI: Michigan State University research report.

Sower, Christopher, John Holland, Kenneth Tiedke, and Walter Freeman
1957   *Community Involvement: The Webs of Formal and Informal Ties That Make for Action*. Glencoe, IL: The Free Press.

Spates, James L., and John J. Macion
1982   *The Sociology of Cities*. New York: St. Martin's Press.

Spiegel, Hans B.C.
1969   "Issues That Trigger Participation." In *Citizen Participation in Urban Development, Vol. II—Cases/Programs*. Washington, DC: NTL Institute for Applied Behavioral Science.

Spiegel, Hans B.C., and Stephen D. Mittenthal
1968   "The Many Faces of Citizen Participation: A Bibliographic Overview." In *Citizen Participation in Urban Development, Vol. 1—Concepts and Issues*, edited by Hans B.C. Spiegel. Washington DC: NTL Institute for Applied Behavioral Science.

Taylor, H. Ralph
1969   "Citizen Participation in the Model Cities Program." In *Citizen Participation in Urban Development, Vol. II—Cases and Programs*, edited by Hans B.C. Spiegel. Washington DC: NTL Institute for Applied Behavioral Science.

Tinder, Glenn
1980   *Community Reflections on a Tragic Ideal.* Baton Rouge: Louisiana State University Press.

Tonnies, Ferdinand
1988   *Community and Society.* Translated by Charles P. Loomis. New Brunswick, NJ: Transaction Books.

Turk, Herman
1977   "Interorganizational Networks in Urban Society: Initial Perspectives and Comparative Research." In *Social Networks*, edited by Samuel Leinhardt. New York: Academic Press.

Utterback, James M.
1974   "Innovation in Industry and the Diffusion of Technology." *Science* 183:620-626.

Warren, Roland L.
1963   *The Community in America.* Chicago: Rand McNally.

1972   *The Community in America*, 2nd edition. Chicago: Rand McNally.

Weber, Max
1943   *Economic Organization.* Translated by A.M. Henderson and Talcott Parsons. New York: Oxford University Press.

Weiss, Robert S., and Eugene Jacobson
1955   "A Method for the Analysis of the Structure of Complex Organizations." *American Sociological Review* 20 (August):661-668.

Whitehead, A. N.
1933   *Science and the Modern World.* London: Cambridge University Press.

Wild, R. A.
1981   *Australian Community Studies and Beyond*. Sydney: George
            Allen and Unwin.

Wilke, Henki A.M., ed.
1985   *Coalition Formation*. Amsterdam: Elsevier Science Publ.

Williams, A.R.
1989   "Chicago's Hancock Center." *Journal of the National
            Geographic Society* 175, 22:175-185.

Young, Michael
1988   *The Metronomic Society: Natural Rhythms and Human
            Time Tables*. Cambridge: Harvard University Press.

Zaltman, Gerald, et al.
1973   *Innovations and Organizations*. New York: John Wiley and
            Sons.

Zorbaugh, Harvey W.
1929   *The Gold Coast and the Slum*. Chicago: University of
            Chicago Press.

1929   "Transcendental Dialectic." In *The Critique of Pure Reason*,
            edited by Norman Travis and Kemp Smith. London:
            Macmillan and Co.